1

Prateek Kanchan

Writings on Marketing: Research Journey of an academician from 2002 to 2015

Kindle publishing

Preface

It is important for a researcher to promote his research for the benefit of new researchers as well as society so that benefit accrues to all the stakeholders in the society. Moreover, when the researcher is a Professor in Higher Management Education, this becomes much more important. It is with this intention and commitment that I decided to bring to this world the papers which I have presented at various National and International Conferences, and which were not published by the organizers of these conferences. At the most, a small abstract of these papers were published in the book of abstracts which they called as souvenir, or book of abstracts. So, I am here with this book consisting of my papers which were not published but presented at various National and International Conferences, majorly in India, and one outside India.

Any book which is written involves a lot of support from a host of important people in the life of the author. I strongly feel that this book would not have come out without the support and constant motivation of my father, mother, my wife, and my brother. My extended family members including elders and cousins also played a role in contributing towards the book. On the professional front, Gujarat University in general and B.K.School of Business Management, in particular played a very positive role in making me find time for this work. A Professor is incomplete without good students and alumni. I give due credit to many of my former students who contributed in the form of the material for the book. I also feel indebted to the entire editorial team of Kindle publishing for their guidance from time to time in making the book see the light of the day. However, any error found in the book will be completely unintentional, and I offer unconditional apology for the same, in advance. Happy reading to one and all.

Dr Prateek Kanchan

<table>
<tr><td>Contents</td><td>Pages</td></tr>
</table>

1. Marketing---A Discipline which is fascinating as well as challenging

(This paper was presented as a detailed conceptual paper at Nirma International Conference On Management – 2002 (NICOM-2002), organized by Nirma Institute of Management, Ahmedabad, India during Jan 3-6,2002).

There are lots & lots of statements ,views & opinions about marketing & each of these is debatable by virtue of being subjective in nature. Marketing professionals themselves do not agree most of the times on these aspects. Precisely ,because of this ,there is always a room for controversy surrounding   Marketing as a discipline. Its controversial nature makes it challenging as well as fascinating to all those concerned as well as unconcerned. Whether we go deep into the Environment of Marketing ,Consumer Buying Behavior or Industrial Buying Behavior, New Product Development, Advertising & Promotion Management, Sales & Distribution Management, Pricing, Branding , Market Research etc., the challenge is everywhere.

Firms all over the world unearth, analyze & act upon a number of trends which give a direction to their marketing activities in short as well as long run. For example, when a research on the buying behavior of a section of consumers is undertaken, it gives a response which relates to their habits , likes , dislikes, tastes, whims, & fancies etc of all of them. Findings of a sample of such consumers are extrapolated to come to a figure of demand for a particular product in the entire market   which the company wants to address. Thereafter, the company comes up with the production plan, inventory plans, warehousing, transportation plans, marketing strategies etc., implement them & reap profits over a period of time.

Now marketers come for some criticism here. Consumers complain that they are intruded into their personal time, get phone calls at odd hours, are followed by researchers in office etc. But in order to ensure mutual benefit to consumers as well as the company, such things should be taken for granted by the consumers & the researchers should also try to minimize inconvenience to consumer. All this give & take is essential if the consumer wants a satisfying product & to ensure no any cribbing from him later on about the company not taking him into confidence before developing & launching the product.

In a similar manner, New Product Development exercise is a strong area for congruence between the company's policy makers, marketing personnel, & the consumers including the entire supply chain till the end-user. No new product can be developed in an ivory tower. This new product can be new for the company or new for the market in which it is operating or something revolutionary brought out for the first time & never before heard in history. Whatever may be the marketing strategy for the new product depending upon its type, Lovelock,a well known writer on New Product Development says that the entire New Product Development exercise should begin with a review of the company's corporate objectives & pass through different phases till the product is introduced. This again highlights the importance of research & innovation without vitiating from the corporate objectives. It is ridiculous to say that marketers force their products on unwilling consumers by sweet talk without going into their actual needs & wants. In fact marketers undertake a lot of pains & find out through research, the requirements of consumers & then approach them with a strategy along with the product which the consumer likes.

But, as there is a darker side to every issue, same can be said about marketing. At the same time , it is not the discipline of Marketing per se which is bad, but some practitioners & promoters at times commit blunders thereby bringing the whole subject area into disrepute. It has to be corrected & I'm all for it. I'll now be highlighting certain examples where marketing acquired a bad name & the question of ethics came into picture. Who can forget the Tuffs shoe advertisement by Phoenix in mid-90s in which Milind Soman & Madhu Sapre were shown entwined with almost nothing to cover their bodies except a snake swirling all over them besides sporting a pair of the shoe advertised. It created a hue & cry & ultimately the objectionable parts of the print ad were covered in the future releases in magazines etc. This ad tried to promote a product by using sex appeal & that too in an obscene manner. We also find companies fighting over ethical issues & later on agree to bury the issue as well as ethics itself thereby caring a damn for the consumer. The classic example in this direction is that of a case between HLL & Fena on the detergent bar which showed how both the companies levelled charges on one another's promotions on television, making a big issue of 'ethical concern for the end-user' & even taking one another to court thereby making consumers feel important. But,just when consumers started feeling important ,both the companies agreed to settle the matter 'amicably' & bury the hatchet ,thereby letting ethics go to dogs. Another very significant issue here is the public concern. 1997 was a watershed year for the roads & road-users of Delhi. Supreme Court got convinced of the strong relationship between the number of accidents on Delhi roads & the hoardings of all sizes with ads of different companies almost choking the skyline of our National Capital. These hoardings were banned & long continuous stretch of the Ring Road started giving a good drive & uninterrupted flow of traffic to Delhi-ites with their mind & eyes becoming free of any distraction. The number of accidents also got reduced dramatically. By quoting these examples, I mean to say that the activity of marketing & the work of marketers is welcome but it should be accompanied with a responsibility & concern for the society. Otherwise, there are a lot of sticks with which we as marketers can be made responsible e.g., consumer forum, courts etc.

2. MANAGING BRANDS:

RELEVANCE OF CONVENTIONAL WAYS

(This paper was presented at Nirma International Conference On Management (NICOM 2003)

organized by Nirma Institute of Management, Ahmedabad, India during JANUARY 2-4, 2003).

Branding as the name suggests is a process which makes sure that a product or service of significance to a very large number of users gets established in their psyche and remains there for a long period of time and if possible forever, thereby not only purchased/used by them regularly but many others are encouraged by them to purchase/use it frequently. In order to do so, the companies resort to many tools straight from the books besides applying innovations from time to time. There are n number of examples which can support the use of one or a judicious mix of more than one tool in order to ensure that a brand stands the test of rapidly changing times. We'll profile the various tools of branding and see the application of these tools at different times in order to critically analyze them.

Profiling Consumer behavior*: Studying consumer behavior has all along remained the foundation for any exercise in branding. What is important here is the way in which this profiling is done in order to find out the leads for brand positioning.

Quality of output/service: Quality is something which will always remain with a product. Now, getting feedback from the market on a regular basis which guides the overall company efforts in the direction of upgrading the quality goes a long way in managing brands. Either, the company's product quality is bad or the quality of marketing is lacking or any other qualitative aspect or even a mix of all or some of them. Professional handling of these feedback/s helps the company to come out of any morass in which it might have landed or was about to land. But all this can be done provided the whole organizational system is one in thinking.

Internet promotion: In order to make effective use of the internet in the direction of building and promoting brands, the companies should be clear about the reasons for using net in branding. It may be to sell products(e-commerce) or build the brand(i-branding), or to save money(e-operation) etc. Once the objective is clear, the company can effectively use this tool to make the brand loud and clear in promoting itself. According to ICFAI Research Center, there are certain specific reasons for advertising on the internet. These include a sizable shift in time spent from TV viewing to Internet by PC users, profile of internet users matching with the desired target audience who are mostly well educated belonging to a high income group, reach of internet across the globe is at much lower cost as compared to TV, updating ads is easy and frequently possible with minimal cost and communication can be interactive and engaging on the net etc. But, the site should be attractive to make the customer visit it frequently and stay longer every time he or she visits it and also comes back again. Companies advertise in print, audio-visual as well as audio media besides billboards and hoardings etc to drive traffic towards the website and sustain it again and again. The emphasis should lie on how best to use the potential of the Net to develop an ongoing two-way dialogue with the consumer, rather than posting standard information on the site that resembles a brochure.

Printed word: Public relations play an important role in promoting a brand. In PR, the printed word plays a very significant role. Whether it is apart of an advertisement or the verbatim speech of the company's CMD at its annual general body meeting or even a press release , anything done should be highly professional keeping in mind the existing position of the brand in the market as well as the future which the company intends to command. When an ad copy is written, one needs to focus on the customer more than the product. The customer is the one with the money as well as the need. It may require writing copy that appeals to emotions and solves problems. Most statistics claim that it takes about 7 impressions before a customer even notices an ad.

Words on the audio-visual media: Lot of wards have been said about the advertising on Television. What is of special mention here is that care should be taken to find the right words and convey these words in the right context. It can continue unchanged for decades eg., Pan Parag, Godrej storewel etc or it can change at regular intervals viz., Intel, Raymonds, Coca-cola etc. Utmost care should be taken before releasing anything to the audio-visual media as millions see it, recall it and even base there decisions on it.

The power of colors: Colors play a lot of role in making a brand accepted, recalled and identified with a multitude of regions, countries, people and blocs. With a deft use of these color and color combinations, any brand can significantly upgrade its position in the market or maintain its existing position.

The game of name: It is often said that what is their in a name. But, a brand can entrench itself in the consumers perceptible mind by having a name which makes its position secure and with initial ups and down, the name carries it along forward for long times to come.

Programming sales incentives: It is very important to program incentives to sales persons in such a way that branding exercise gets a momentum at the bottom rung. This gets done better when an established brand name does a brand extension and makes sales incentive plan attractive. ICICI Bank went ahead with getting bank accounts opened in all categories by giving good monetary as well as non-monetary incentives to all its sales representatives for every account opened through them.

Musical scores: It is often found that music is as symbolic in association with us as brands. Sometimes, it is because of the music that we remember the brand through its advertisement. It has proved to be a time tested tool whether it is an FMCG or a Consumer Durable or even a service. Examples are numerous viz., Amul, Hajmola, NECC etc.

Using strategic outdoor locations: Outdoor advertising is a part of out-of home media, which are designed almost exclusively to serve only an advertising function and include billboards, transit advertising and posters in public places. In India, while ad spends are reportedly being slashed across all categories, outdoors has always remained a cheaper option compared to other media.

Employee as an ambassador: In any company, brand building exercise will come to a full circle provided every employee possesses a feeling of belongingness to the brand. It will be futile for the company to engage in branding exercise where only a department and employees within it are assigned to make the brand a success. In fact, every employee in any department or discipline should be made to feel good and emotional about the brand so that whenever required, a positive word of mouth, a favorable action etc comes out of him or her. It will ensure that the brand is rejuvenated continuously and possess corporate backing.

Customer Relationship Management: The present day business activity lays a lot of emphasis on the concept of customer relationship management. However, many times it comes out to be lip service and nothing more. This needs to change. In companies, where this is done, huge amount of money is spent and manpower is made responsible to ensure customer orientation. With this, the whole brand gets a face-lift. In order to do so, the company has to ensure that all this is practiced within the company so that relationship building, interpersonal relationships etc get smoothened and it becomes a normal routine. Many times, what happens is that lot of emphasis is given to forging and nurturing CRM with all the stages of Supply Chain but inside the company, no one sees eye to eye on most of the issues. In other words, it requires improving the culture of the work place, empowering employees as individuals as well as teams besides making them feel as if they own their responsibilities.

 Fortunately, many companies have realized and implemented   all these activities and are continuously improving on these.

There are lots of things which can be said about branding as an important tool of over-all marketing. But everything has to be looked into from the point of view of application. As long as application works, branding will remain successful for all times to come.

3.Advertising Cosmetics: A strategic shift

(This paper was presented as a detailed analytical paper at Nirma International Conference On Management – 2003 (NICOM-2003), organized by Nirma Institute of Management, Ahmedabad, India during Jan 2-4,2003).

In the world of marketing, a product category which has attracted maximum attention is cosmetics. This attention has multiplied with the expansion of the various type of modified products and launch of certain new products at different times. It has also been noticed that we as individuals have accepted as well as rejected a number of body care products from time to time depending upon the changes in our perception due to some or other reasons. It is the plethora of these reasons which have either been introduced by advertisers to stimulate perceptions in the masses or due to the presence of these reasons, marketers and advertisers have promoted their cosmetics according to their convenience. Moreover, this convenience generates appreciation, ethical dilemmas as well as controversies while promoting various brands. This entire exercise leads to a lot of learning for sponsors about what might have gone wrong on the advertising front besides what could be further improved depending upon the feedback of the ads released. In this direction, let us scan some advertisements of certain cosmetic products released over a period of time and try to infer the reasons behind them as well as the leads which they can generate.

1] **New Margo:** This all purpose cream advertisement says 'My skin has no secrets….just natural care from Margo'.The copy further highlights that its rich and non-greasy with the unique combination of Neem and Aloe Vera. The natural goodness of Neem keeps the skin blemish-free while Aloe Vera moisturises and nourishes the skin ,leaving it smooth ,healthy and glowing naturally.The ad shows a beautiful female face which matches with all this copy. The ad directly addresses the

expectation of every female to look beautiful and also explains how to go about doing it. It also carefully tries to invite any criticism normally associated with chemical based cosmetic creams or lotions. Moreover, it directly tries to leverage the advantage of the name 'Margo' which has become synonymous with herbal and chemical free skin care soap. All this forces the reader or viewer to think, discuss or ask someone to support or reject all or some of the contentions advertised.

2] **Lakme:** This is the one brand which has ruled the heart of a number of females since decades. This name is associated with a number of categories viz., fairness cream, sunscreen lotion, nail enamel, lipstick, moisturizer, perfumed nail enamels, deep pore products etc. The ads for all these products say something which project what the sponsor wants to achieve besides giving some lead to would be advertisers as well as consumers. For example Lakme deep pore products ad copy shows the way to uncover yourself by using shine control cleanser for 30 seconds in the morning, cleansing pads for 30 seconds during the day and cleansing milk for 30 seconds in the night. The ad explains that due to the pressure of work at different times of the day,a lady needs to clean her face accordingly and one product is not sufficient for all times. By depicting a beautiful face in the ad copy, the ad tries to sell three products at the same time. The print ad which got repeated in The Times of India and other newspapers and magazines regularly tries to come closer to the consumer by using convenience and time platform. In the same way, Lakme tried to make nail paints more interesting by putting perfume in them and promoting them as an invention where perfume combines with nail paints. It is a novel idea to add glamour to an otherwise common product. Moreover it continuously highlights its range of colors thereby pampering the modern female for her appetite for variety in beauty products. Lakme's Maximum Moisturizer is not a very new product but its recent print ads show a beautiful lady glowing because of it and a muscled man reaching out from a portrait to her with the one line copy saying 'Skin so smooth, it's irresistible'. It highlights that the desire of a young lady to attract attention of the opposite sex gets fulfilled by this brand. New Sunscreen Lotion from Lakme promotes itself by highlighting qualitative as well as quantitative benefits over its earlier skin-care products. Again, a beautiful female face tries to prove the point. Same is the case with its Fair Perfect Cream which highlights the road to perfection through fairness. All along this huge gamut of products from Lakme portfolio, the consumer needs to be educated because he or she is bound to get confused as almost every offering tries to target skin-care. The company will be best advised to ensure that its one product does not cannibalize sale of the other one eg., fairness cream and sunscreen lotion. Moreover the company should not drive home the point that dark face color can be changed to fair one by using a particular cream as such a statement is not only in bad taste but also demeaning to that very section of female consumers which are its main buyers. Instead, what is stopping a big brand name like Lakme to bring out products and promote them in such a way where the dark color of the skin goes along well with skin care? Or Lakme is trying to say that dark color women are not beautiful if they don't change their color?My answer is no and I'm ready to argue on that.

3] **L'OREAL Paris :** Hair colorant as a product category used to be known in this country only through a number of hair dyes . Moreover, hair coloring did not develop in India except for some special occasions and that too confined to some section of people. Any player in this category has to be very careful in promoting its brands. This is what L'OREAL Paris has done. Its three print ads in the Times of India dated 08/07/2001,12/08/2001 and 03/03/2002 aptly tell the same story. In fact, the very nature of the language used in the ads, the models used as brand ambassadors etc are all pointing in that direction. The copy explains how to protect your hair while using a colorant and tries to remove all doubts in readers mind about harmful effects of coloring. The copy further endorses its hair care plank by explaining the ceramide and protein contents along with a double dose of conditioner. Its choice of models viz., Diana Hayden and Claire Forlani appears to be very careful as one of their claim to fame is beautiful hairs for which they can go to any length. All said and done, certain points are worth noting. Firstly, average Indian consumer where the potential lies has to be educated about the benefits of hair coloring, options available in this direction and how to use such products. Secondly, apart from the endorsement from celebrities, the companies can supplement it by a sales promotion where a small quantity is distributed to a sample of users in select regions for testing over a period of time and their feedback collected after that. Here the company can also commit reasonable compensation to any user if anything goes wrong to her after using the product. This may be time consuming but at the end of it, the company becomes more closer to its prospective users and it can highlight these findings in further ads to broad-base its range.

4] **New International Lux Skincare**: Lux is that offering from the cosmetic stable of our country which has become synonymous with beauty soap. In fact the company itself must have realized that instead of a mere soap company, why not position itself as a skincare company with a range of products. But it also believes that a range does not mean a score of different products launched at the same time. It very carefully expanded its portfolio by adding body wash along with soap in three different varieties if we go by its first print ad in The Times of India dated 20/01/2002 and thereafter. The varieties are moisturizing body wash and soap, Deep cleansing body wash and soap and Sun protection face wash and soap. Further it explains the contents and usefulness of all the categories. The copy shows Aishwarya Rai looking straight into the eyes of the reader lying by the side of the entire range with the caption 'It's not just soap, it's skincare'. What the advertisement lacks is the clear-cut strategy for the masses.If the range is targeted for a niche, it appears fine but there also the lady needs to be educated the specific reasons for using or not using which body wash and soap at what time. If the ad projects the use of all the categories depending upon different times of the day, that sends a message to the readers to have the whole category in their bathrooms. Here the company should very well understand that in the niche segment, there is a straight competition from deodorants which prevents the lady from taking bath so often while giving her a feeling of freshness at the same time. The company will be better served if it educates the users and prospective users also about the benefits of taking baths at different times of the day along with the features, contents of its various offerings.

5] **Sunsilk** : This brand has almost become synonymous with the shampoo category. It did not do anything drastically to alter its image as a shampoo manufacturer but it dabbled with adding hair colorant in its product portfolio. It also advertised its Fruitamins way back in 1999.. One print ad for fruitamin as hinted above had a copy which went like this:**What's a girls secret for hair that is full of body and bounce? It's Sunsilk Fruitamins.Full of the goodness of Fruitamins, vitamins from fruit extracts.Sunsilk Fruitamins gives your hair more bounce and volume,and makes it more and more beautiful, wash after wash.** I have not seen many ads or promotion of it further and the reason is quite simple. The use of egg yolk and other conventional raw inputs in imparting life to the hairs is so common that selling a brand as a vitamin carrying stuff and not calling it a shampoo will create a nagging doubt about its utility. The message is quite simple that it is better to act smart and straight then to be oversmart. Sunsilk would have been better served by bringing out different varieties of shampoos and call them shampoos only instead of fruitamins. An ad worth appreciating from Sunsilk appeared in The Times of India 13/05/2001 which showed four female models rejoicing to have that particular Sunsilk brand of shampoo which suits their hairs.It clearly informed the readers the variety available leaving upon them to choose from it. Taking cue from L'OREAL or vice-versa, Sunsilk also came up with a print ad in The times of India 22/07/2001 which promoted hair colorants as the female model was shown playing with cans of all the seven colors which resembled cans of Lactogen. Since then I've not come across any more of its advertising which clearly showed Sunsilk trying to dabble in a new category and then going silent on it. In fact, it is a wise decision if we go by the book "FOCUS-The future of your company depends on it" by Al Ries.

6] **Maybelline:** Oil control make-ups, Nail Enamels, Lip-Sticks and Pencils are all in the family as far as Maybelline,New York is concerned.It uses the words 'may be' to create an affinity with the brand name itself. through its numerous ads. Sheetal Mallar and Josie Maran have been modeling from April 2001 in its print ads. In the first ad on 08/04/2001 in The Times of India Maybelline announced the introduction of 'must be magic' depicting lip-stick and nail enamel thereby making an entry with words like shimmering, spellbound, magical , mystical etc. Over a month later on 20/05/2001, it informed the readers through the same newspaper,the introduction of Shine Free Oil Control Make-Up highlighting its shine-stopping formulas with a beaming face of Sheetal Mallar wearing it. Then with a gap of over six months, on 16/12/2001 and 23/12/2001, it again advertised nail enamels and lip-sticks being sported by Josie .Although it introduced it again, but this time it compared both these with wine and divinity.Again, Josie was shown on 10/02/2002 promoting Maybelline Cool Effect cooling cream eyecolor in tube and pencil form.Then again, on 17/03/2002, the company advertised Wet shine Lip-sticks carrying Vitamin-E and available in 10 translucent shades with wine shade being sported by who else than Josie Maran. So, the cycle goes

4. SERVICES MARKETING: A DIASPORA OF STRATEGIES AND TACTICS

(This paper was presented at Fifth National Conference on " Changing Trends in Management-Challenges and Opportunities" Prestige Institute of Management and Research , 2, Education & Health Sector, Scheme 54, Indore (M.P)-452010 INDIA during January 30-31,2003)

Service as the name suggests has got a lot to do with the word 'Serve'. In fact, a whole mentality works behind making any service offering attractive and worth spending money on. All service providers have been adopting a plethora of strategies and tactics in order to ensure their position in this world of competition. They very well know that with time, this competition will increase manifold and they'll be there in the race only if they use innovative strategies which stand the test of changing times and which are regularly changed depending upon new requirements from time to time. In the recent past, in-fact since the latter part of 1990s service organizations have adopted all types of measures to ward away competition. This might have been in the form of better facilities, improved communications, deft handling of complaints , variety of offerings with some or the other benefit attached etc. In-fact, they do it and position their brands as strong caretakers of the society and nation at times. If we look at marketing of services, sector wise, we'll find that, diasporas will become visible on their own. Some of these sectors are as follows:

Education: A variety of activities are done in order to market all types of education offered by the private sector for various levels. It has been written and appreciated by many on the one hand as well as criticized by many others on the other hand. But the marketers of this very essential service have exploited one basic fact related to education and that is the unavailability of state run avenues to all aspirants of education. This made this area a fertile ground for private sector to apply all business tools and tricks as applied to consumer durables as well as fast moving consumer goods and other services. Many times, it results in promotional wars as is experienced in any other product. At times, this goes unchecked and lands the promoters into troubles which could be legal, financial and emotional. But, many educational institutions are careful in advertising their courses, infrastructure, Unique Selling Propositions(USPs), placement records etc. This aspect has come into the ambit of lot of debate specially because of education related to Management, Information Technology, Engineering, Medical Sciences etc (basically professional).

Tourism: Tourism relates to a country, its location, its history, its people, the gifts which it has acquired from nature, the systems, law and order which prevails within its boundaries etc. Now, all those organizations which ensure the flow of tourist traffic inwards as well as outwards with respect to a country, region etc through their human resources, liaisons, physical assets etc are forming a strong service sector which can make or break the image of a country as a tourist destination for leisure as well as business traveler. Moreover, billions of rupees are made by service providers in this sector. All the strategies and tactics required to market their offerings are resorted to with impunity from time to time. Whether it is a travel agency or a state government or even government of India, attracting tourists from within the country or from abroad is done by using all the elements of marketing mix. If Goa positions itself through its virgin beaches and magnificent churches, lush forests and variety of sea food etc, Gujarat positions itself through its link with our freedom struggle, name of Gandhiji and Sardar Patel, heritage sites of Dwarka, Somnath temple, Sabarmati Ashram etc.

Travel agencies try to be one up over their rivals by offering attractive packages, durational discounts, raffle coupons etc. In all these exercises, there is a common thread which runs all through and that is the promotion of a package which includes the place (country, region etc),price(fares, discount etc) and promotion(advertising, schemes, selling etc). Many times, all these strategies and tactics get affected negatively due to certain unexpected developments like communal riots, natural calamities, diplomatic hurdles etc. Providers of tourism services have to make extra efforts in order to ensure that the trust which a traveler or prospective traveler has reposed in its area of operation does not wane much due to such negative developments. Although it takes time, but this is the precise moment when these people have to work hard in order to rectify the damage for which they are not at all responsible.

Health care: Health used to be treated as a service confined to only Government clinics and doctors as late as mid eighties. These were the places where people normally dreaded to go as their up-keep, the ambience etc made anyone going for treatment more sick. I'm not talking about premium hospitals for elite class of patients which were existing and were having there own business. Private health-care for masses of all classes at an affordable price got into services sector in a big way from early 1990s. All these private hospitals got into the act of marketing there services using all the conventional as well as novel tools of marketing. Qualified and experienced Doctors, infrastructure, connectivity etc were highlighted in

advertisements and promotions in order to generate business. Offcourse, charges continue to be hefty, but a strong segment which possesses the affordability for such treatment is identified, targeted and continuously wooed for business. Here, the number of patients(read customers) is less but every patient belongs to upper or upper middle class, maintaining database is easy, which makes targeting and subsequent wooing also easy. Mass market advertising is done albeit on a low scale to generate business from class/es who are migrating upwards into upper middle or upper classes regularly.

Air travel: This sector is a very important part of the overall service industry. It involves domestic as well as international travel. As far as strategies and tactics are concerned, it revolve around offering schemes related to particular routes at particular times, pricing discounts during certain flights, increasing comforts of various types while flying etc. Competition gets hot when all the players resort to similar schemes from time to time. This precisely is the reason why many private airlines in India have wound up in the late 1990s after making a grand entry in early 1990s. For almost a decade, domestic travelers were wooed by almost half a dozen airlines with scheme after scheme. Ultimately, that did not last long and most of these airlines started feeling the pressure and returns were not coming anymore. In India, still a sizeable section of domestic travelers use train journey even if this entails time. They manage their time accordingly. Marketers of Air travel in private sector have to convince the traveler of the value of time even if it requires a high price to be paid. All promotions should go in this direction as other aspects are only secondary. Off-course, there is a limit to reducing prices, so there is no point to target some classes of people. Same can be said

about international travel.

Rail transport: Although rail transport has gone through lots of ups and downs in the recent past, but it has come up with good and educative communications as far as promoting itself is concerned. But, one thing is sure that the accidents which are taking place with an alacrity which is growing over time pose serious challenge to its image. It should realize soon that its greeting to every ticket holder for his /her safe journey has to be translated in action.

Hotels and Restaurants: With competition coming in every field, hospitality field cannot remain aloof from consistently marketing itself. Burgeoning campaigns, hosting of important events, bringing out special packages for guests, sponsoring events etc are resorted to by hotels and restaurants from time to time. But ,in case of hotels whether star or non-star, what matters is the occupancy levels which need to be increased even when numbers of hotels have increased. Keeping this in mind, many hotels of all levels have decreased their tariffs and brought them down to very low levels as compared to high standards set earlier. Restaurants take advantage of locations, special items, weekend offerings etc which keep on changing rapidly as well as regularly. It is required as in a stretch of one kilometer, where there was only one restaurant earlier, now almost five exist with a whole lot of offerings perched up.

Entertainment: When we talk of entertainment, a host of things come to our mind ranging from films, serials on TV, sports shows etc. Let us confine our discussion to in-house entertainment .In the recent past, it has been found that makers of serials in all channels have tried to portray household relationships as a USP. It was good in the beginning when some were doing it but when every one started doing it, no more it remained a USP and it actually has become a distraction now. But, in order to re-generate this interest, these promoters and producers are linking prizes in cash and kind with their serials which keeps the interest of some avid viewers intact continuously. All these producers and directors should keep in mind that with cable revolution well entrenched in India now, switching loyalties of viewers first and sponsors afterwards is not difficult. In this situation, it is better to end a particular serial in time before it is hated and booed out by people and make a new one with a contemporary script to generate new interest for a new period of time.

Banking and Finance: The area which has seen the most sophisticated use and application of marketing strategies in the recent past has been banking and finance. Players in this arena are bigwigs in their own light and when you have names like ICICI, HDFC, IDBI, UTI and many others, the arena becomes a virtual service marketing warfare. All these names have already existed in their core area of financial services in the past and they are now leveraging the brand equity built through that to be used in Retail Banking, Mutual funds and   Insurance. Uptill now, it is going smoothly as Indian consumers in ever increasing numbers have taken well the concept of private retail banking. Consequently, the number of accounts are increasing rapidly in these banks and financial institutions. All the players in this arena will sustain in the long run only if the service levels are maintained and no any slack is shown in this regard. Off-course, initially, it all has come as a pleasant surprise to all account holders after having gone through the drudgery of getting served(if I'm using the write word) by most of the nationalized banks or LIC etc.

Telecom: In the recent times, telecommunication services have gone into an overdrive with a lot of companies trying to play a lot of games in trying to come closer to the customer. Mainly speaking, this has come to be known as brand wars when we talk in the context of mobile telephony. Ultimately, the customer has derived benefit out of it by asking and getting quality service, changing service provider at will, paying a very reasonable price in various schemes and options available. Service providers in this category are all names to reckon with viz., Airtel, Hutchison, Idea, BSNL etc., and many more to come. Initially, barring BSNL, all service providers due to the huge costs related to infrastructure development, clearances etc, had to charge a high price from their subscribers which ensured that mobile telephony remained a premium service to be used by upper class elite or company sponsored professionals. Once, the initial costs were covered, and essential requirements were in place, only variable costs were to be charged on a case to case to case basis which made the price of this service fall sharply and now it has become a service which even middle class can afford. These service providers are using all tools to be one up on others in order to get more and more subscribers. They have come very close to the customer through their SMS(short messaging services) which I feel is a master stroke in taking them closer to the customer. Anyway, the war is on and communication has become more savvy, modern, and fast. With time, we as customers will be wooed again by new tools.

Through the discussion of certain sectors, I feel that strategies and tactics are there and will continue to remain there with changes from time to time which can be minor or major. The aspect which is of utmost importance is to sustain in the market in the face of competition which is only going to increase in monstrous proportions in times to come.

5. Managing individuals qualitatively: An ethical paradox in Organizations

(This paper was presented at National Conference on " Ethical Management in Organizations" March 15 & 16, 2003, at Department of Business Administration, Bhavnagar University,Bhavnagar-364002 (Gujarat), India)

It requires a very holistic approach when a delicate issue like managing individuals in organizations is concerned. We have to look at it from certain precise angles. These angles are as follows

1] **Employee**: The term employee also requires to be dissected threadbare in order to present a viable analysis. This means the various functions an individual performs as an employee at his/her workplace

a. Peer : Although in a peer group, an individual is at par with his/her peers but there are certain acts on the part of the peers which can hamper the work of the individual. Now these acts may or may not be intentional but as long as the individual's work gets affected negatively, these should be avoided. Now, those who organized this disturbance derive certain benefit out of it, which of course is at the cost of the individual's career. But, as there is no way to check, control or curb such an activity, it goes on and the management also allows it to happen and the individual who suffers due to it either accepts it as his/her fate or starts applying it on others. In this way, either it remains one way traffic or it becomes free for all. In any way, the company suffers as it takes away lot of man-hours of productive work. The organizational intelligence network should be on a constant alert so that such acts get detected as early as possible and remedial measures applied. It may be found that the initiators were themselves frustrated due to some reasons and instead of taking it straight to the people who mattered , they started creating same situations for those who

were having no problems with their work and were not frustrated. This organizational
intelligence network should be created after a thorough process of screening, interviews etc so
that unbiased and impartial people become a part of it. Otherwise, the whole purpose of
organizational intelligence will get killed.

b. Subordinate: The subordinate discussed here is with respect to the individual who is the
focus of this discussion (executive). There is a normal tendency among any subordinate to look
at the minus-points of the superior and the executive has to accept and work towards removing
that mental block. At times, it may so happen that the individual inadvertently acts in an
irresponsible manner which hurts or damages the reputation of the subordinate. In some other
scenario, another subordinate jealous of his colleague's good rapport with the executive starts
creating suspicion in the mind of his/her colleague in order to create a rift between the two and
then pitch in as the executive's well-wisher thereby taking himself/herself in the good books of
the executive and getting his colleague side-lined. The individual(executive) has to be vary of all
these games which a subordinate plays against another subordinate. All this does not mean that
strictness can be ignored. In fact, strictness and discipline can co-exist with a humane treatment
towards subordinate/s where the possibility of human error/s at times does not constitute a
reprimand always.

c. Superior : The superior to the executive discussed here plays a significant role as   far as
ethical treatment towards the executive is concerned. Most importantly, the superior has to lead
by example and show all those features in himself/herself which are expected from the
subordinate. Only then, can he/she command respect from the subordinate(executive) which
alone could ensure ethical conduct towards the subordinate. At times, the superior has to guide
the subordinate in order to come out from some personal problems in order to get work done.

Normally, the superiors avoid getting into this, but when it starts taking a toll on the efficiency of the subordinate, the superior should be able to intelligently figure it out ,carefully intervene and bring the subordinate back to confidence while working. Many companies encourage this approach as it not only helps in making a subordinate feel comfortable, but it also makes him/her more loyal and committed towards the organization. It also helps the superior not to make discrimination among different subordinates on the basis of sycophancy. A subordinate who is not involved in sycophancy but works in a committed manner should be taken seriously by the superior as compared to the one who is doing nothing but involved only in sycophancy. More important is the ability of the superior to differentiate between the

two. Of-course it requires a superior to be very honest and not guided by prejudice at any point of time. Any executive will love to have such a boss. This fair treatment towards the executive should go beyond symbolic, emotional and personal guidance and get reflected in the executive's confidential reports, progression recommendations, salary hikes etc. At no point of time, a growing executive should be taken as a threat by the superior. Instead, it should make him/her feel to start taking higher responsibilities and move at higher positions with new and challenging responsibilities. In other words, a growing executive should be taken as an opportunity by the superior rather than a threat .

2] Employer: The company which is the employer has to be very profound and clear in its ethical conduct. In the pursuit of monetary goals and targets which come under tremendous pressure from time to time, concern for ethical conduct takes a back seat and all human aspects get relegated to the background. Now, the employee(executive under consideration) has to be made to feel in-house where he or she can empathize with and gets empathized by others whenever a feeling of isolation or insecurity or career digression etc develops with anyone. The question arises as to who will make that feeling get established. It is also seen that many companies have all these points in print which get circulated across the length and breadth of the organization,. Actually, when the time comes for action, nothing happens and print remains only print. What is more important is to ensure a mechanism where the moment such a problem arises, a senior executive entrusted with ensuring ethical conduct automatically comes to know about it and starts acting on it to bring the executive concerned back to work with his/her dilemma resolved. Now this Mr/Ms Ethical Conductor or Mr/Ms Impartial (whatever we may like to address him/her) can be either a very senior employee or some member of the Board of Governors who is respected by every member of the organization by virtue of his outstanding conduct in the past and not only by virtue of his position . Many times it also happens that although the culture pervading the organization is fine but inadvertently, the organization allows it to be vitiated. At times, due to monetary aspects moving well with the company, non-monetary aspects or ethical considerations get ignored and unknowingly, anyone can get victimized. As the Employer is at the top, all the blame comes to it or its Governing board.

The discussion up-till now focuses on the aspects of what could go wrong from time to time which harms individual growth on ethical grounds. This has got to do with the individual himself/herself as well as his/her subordinate/s besides the colleague/s and also superiors, which ultimately gets capped by the inactivity or insensitivity or at times connivance of the employer also. We need to ponder seriously on the ways and means to control this dilemma from becoming a chaos or generating anarchy in an otherwise beautiful body called organization. These ways and means relate to all the elements of this problem involved.

A] Employee: The employee on his/her part is to ensure that the commitment towards work does not wane as and when he or she finds oneself in an ethical dilemma. On the other hand, his/her efforts towards excellence should get more impetus in order to make it clear that he/she can handle difficult times without affecting productivity negatively. The following elements which constitute the work profile of the employee should apply themselves constructively in order to minimize the ethical dilemma of the employee concerned

a. **Peer**: This person is a colleague at par and he or she should either help in resolving the dilemma or keep aloof. At no point of time, this person should play political games in such situations as it will come a full circle one day and he/she himself/herself will face such a dilemma when the person victimized earlier will play the same game now.

b. **Sub-ordinate:** Instead of developing a cold shoulder towards the superior(executive) the sub-ordinate should work in unison with the senior which not only makes the superior feel comfortable but also the subordinate can learn to grow with a rising executive(superior).

c. **Superior**: The person who is the immediate superior should be careful in dealing with his sub-ordinate professionally as well as personally. This means taking qualitative decisions and making objective judgement whether there is a reward or a punishment .

B] Employer: The organization should all along promote and ensure speedy acceptance and adherence to ethical values among all employees with a strong deterrent for those not following them and a strict punishment also at times when a gross violation takes place. It will get settled down soon when the top people in the organization lead by example.

Conclusion: Although the above discussion tries to bring a qualitative aspect of managing individuals ethically in organizations, but a lot needs to be done in this direction. I'm sure that it serves the purpose of starting an important debate on ethical management of employees by regarding them not as numbers but as good human resources.

6. Advertising for societal benefit leading to Corporate Goodwill

(Certain examples in Indian context)

(This paper was presented at 15th Annual Convention August 22-24,2003 Organized by Association of Indian Management Schools at Xavier Institute of Management, Bhubaneswar, Orissa, India)

Advertising has been consistently used by organizations-profit as well as non-profit to fulfill the desire of promoting there products and services from time immemorial. One of the theme of this conference is 'Corporate Social Responsibility' and this paper will go into this aspect as far as certain genuine causes are concerned. As part of its corporate social responsibility ,when an organization promotes a general cause which transcends the boundaries of region, religion, caste, creed, profession etc, and just thinks about human welfare in all its myriad forms, it clearly shows its genuine concern for human species. The list of such organizations is endless and many of these are known in-general as very strong profit making enterprises ,big as well as small. What makes them think so much about social welfare can be debated but it should be appreciated by all responsible citizens in one voice.

It is very significant that people in general are made aware of the philanthropic concerns which these organizations show through promoting various causes. This makes people recognize their social responsibility as many among them either work with such organizations or they might work with them in future. It is more important when children from very young age require to be guided about their social responsibilities so that by the time they go into their teens, they start understanding the real meaning of becoming a responsible adult. This gives them a foundation on which they can build a strong personality when they start working in various types of organizations.

In this direction, I'll highlight certain print ads which show a strong concern for social welfare. These are a part of the over-all activity performed by the organizations which they represent, in the direction of social responsibility Most of the ads come from Government organizations(big or small), but there are some efforts from the private sector also.

1] Department of Posts:

It smartly highlights various schemes viz., Kisan Vikas Patra, Post Office Monthly Income Scheme, National Savings Certificates, 15-year Public Provident Fund, Five year Recurring Deposit Account and Time Deposit. The headline says " More beneficial, More Secured, Invest in Small Savings". Apart from that , the advertisement goes into explaining the features of the various schemes mentioned above (The Times of India dated 23/03/2002). It is not only promoting the schemes but also persuading readers to put their hard-earned money into time tested instruments in order to reap the benefits for future. Moreover with conditions so amenable to small investor, he or she finds it much more attractive than other sophisticated and modern tools of investment.

2] Pulse Polio Immunization:

Every year this advertisement campaign runs in full steam in all type of media. It basically educates parents of all infants to ensure that Polio drops are given to them. The general perception in an ordinary Indian mindset is that of suspicion towards giving anything oral to a newly born .In-fact ,Ministry of Health and Family Welfare, Govt of India ,through this ad also educates the masses that oral Polio vaccines are perfectly safe as well as necessary(The Times of India dated 30/11/2001,16/01/2002,20/01/2002 and Indian Express dated 01/12/2001). Every year, these ads start appearing from November and go on to the new year month of January, informing and educating people to go for these drops to be carried out on two specific days.Moreover, the Govt also makes sure that all the concerned parents do not find any problem in getting leave on those days, no matter whichever organizations they might be working. This shows the seriousness of the Ministry in making the child healthy. The statistics have shown that as a result of this annual campaign, the infant mortality rate has gone down dramatically.

3] Department of Family Welfare, Ministry of Healthy and Family welfare, Govt of India:

When this body says ' The line separating common cold, cough and pneumonia is as thin as the line between life and death' it is educating parents of newly born to take continuous coughing by their child seriously(The Times of India dated 11/07/2001,02/09/2001,03/09/2001,07/11/2001). The print ad explains the symptoms in very simple language when the child is having a problem in breathing. It is to be noted here that a child of such an age is unable to say anything and with a very less degree of literacy which the parents possess , every second delayed could lead to a tragic fatality.But ,seeing and reading such a message regularly will definitely help millions of such parents and their infants in taking action in time.

4] Indian Railways:

This organization needs no any introduction but its concern towards passenger and freight safety espoused through various ads in the recent past deserves attention and appreciation. It tries to make people responsible by advising them in a simple language to buy tickets from authorized counters/windows and not to buy these from touts and outsiders(The Times of India dated 16/04/2002). In one of its advertisement, Indian Railways calls upon citizens to help in making platforms and compartments beautiful by not littering, using waste-bins and use toilets keeping in mind the convenience of others besides educating others to do the same(The Times of India dated 19/06/2001). All these ads clearly show that the largest public service provider of the masses is adopting all means from time to time in making us more and more responsible. It is required as in spite of all these exhortations many of us do not behave responsibly when we use Railway property or any other public service. One very important concern which has acquired alarming attention of all is the threat of terrorist attacks on the Railway property. Our Railways has tried to educate people to face it intelligently along with the efforts made by Railway authorities. One print ad appearing repeatedly invited citizens to join hands in order to fight RAVANA of terrorism by remaining vigilant for abandoned objects in compartments and on platforms and inform the authorities immediately (The Times of India dated 02/10/2001, 19/06/2001 and India Today Feb 29,1996).

5] Bharat Sanchar Nigam Limited:

This giant of an organization has acquired the image of a monolith in India as far as telecommunications is concerned. A Government of India enterprise, its main service is basic telephony and it added up mobile telephony in its offering from October 2002 across the length and breadth of India. Its print ad says many things e.g., One year old and going places, talking to 2.9 crores, sealing deals mending hearts etc(The Times of India dated 01/10/2001). The advertisement supports each statement with a matching photo. It also mentions in the end 'We don't sell. We Serve'. In short, it can be said that a business objective can easily be served even by clubbing it together and mentioning it alongside a non-business objective.

6] Oil and Natural Gas Corporation Ltd:

Popularly known as ONGC among its employees, suppliers, buyers and common public, this organization has become a strong pillar in the stable of Government of India as a rich and prosperous organization. In the recent past it has advertised its philanthropic concerns at different times viz., World Environment day, Pulse polio campaign, exhorting the masses to be brave while living under fear of terrorism etc.

7] National Literacy Mission:

As part of the world-wide campaign for literacy remembered every year on September 08, International Literacy Day, this organization in its print ad made an impassioned appeal to all concerned to contribute in whichever way possible in order to make India and the World more literate(The Times of India dated 08/09/2001). This mission functioning within Ministry of Human Resource Development informed the readers about its efforts in giving literacy and life-long learning opportunities to all to make India fully literate. It exhorted all of us to help at-least one individual to take the path of literacy and follow it sincerely on International Literacy Day.

8] Narmada Vraksh Utsav-2001:

The print advertisement brought out by Gujarat Government for the 'Plant trees-Greet Narmada' campaign exhorted people that every home must grow a tree as the timing of this Utsav coincided with Narmada water reaching almost every part of Gujarat. It conveyed the message to the masses that the perrennial problem of water shortage in Gujarat has to become a thing of the past and at the same time people should plant more trees, thereby not only welcoming Narmada waters in their backyard but also contributing to more fresh air and soil strength (The Times of India-16/07/2001). The commitment of Gujarat Government was expressed clearly as the names and the photographs of the then Chief Minister ,Forest and Environment Minister, his deputy besides that of Chairman, Sardar Sarovar Narmada Nigam Limited graced the ad copy.

9] Petroleum Conservation Research Association(PCRA):

This organization formed in 1976 advertised heavily in 2001 which was its silver jubilee year. Its print ads showed concern about the depleting quantity of petroleum and the need to conserve it. In one of its ads, it related an individual's nature with the way in which he or she uses petrol where the categories varied from being ignorant on the one end to being farsighted at the other end(The Times of India-18/06/2001).Every right thinking citizen must have got moved by the simple but surely sarcastic language in the ad In one of its ads which got repeated in The Times of India dated 25/05/2001 and 18/06/2001 besides Indian Express dated 25/05/2001,05/06/2001 and 25/06/2001. PCRA invited entries from Owner organizations and Energy consultants based on certain criteria who have done something exemplary in the direction of Energy conservation. On the basis of these entries and further analysis by a highly learned panel of Energy experts , awards were to be given to those entities who really did a good job. Indirectly, these ads motivated people to act decisively and save petrol as much as possible.

10] Environment Pollution Control Authority of NCT:

Here NCT stands for National Capital Territory of Delhi. Way back in 1998, this organization advertised lead-free petrol which only was to be made available at all petrol pumps from September 1,1998 onwards. Its ad campaign conveyed in very straight terms that petrol would no longer be associated with a deadly fluid as its composition has changed .It further said that vehicular pollution would also come down to acceptable levels(The Hindustan Times dated 23/08/1998). The advertisement took special care of the anxiety of all the owners of different types of vehicles about the possibility of their existing engines becoming redundant after this development or those not having catalytic converters have to go for them once petrol becomes lead-free. The ad copy explained these aspects in detail and removed all apprehensions from the minds of the readers. It not only appeared in print but was allover in Delhi on hoardings, kiosks, road-dividers etc. A very good exercise in not only making the air of Delhi pollution free but offsetting any panic among vehicle owners about any negative fall-out of a positive change for society at large.

11] National AIDS Control Organization:

This organization is now active in our country for over two decades ever since the monster of AIDS started showing its first signs of spreading in India. But there are certain advertisements which have touched me as they explain in very simple language the reasons for its spread and the ways to prevent it. One such ad in print said "Sharing needles or syringes for intravenous drugs could be the beginning of your last 'trip'". It further said 'KNOW AIDS FOR NO AIDS'. The detailed ad copy explained various reasons by which AIDS could be contracted thereby warning people to take utmost precaution(Indian Express dated 28/02/1998). These ads have gone a long way in making masses not only aware of this deadly disease but also make them clear that it is only preventable but incurable.

12] Delhi Traffic Police:

One particular exercise and its campaign by this organization was really praiseworthy as its sole aim was to educate Delhi-ites to not only be careful at red light signals but also relax during those periods of traffic halt. As part of Delhi Police Week (Feb 16-22,1998) organized by Delhi Traffic Police, the language used in those print ads explained the pitfalls of driving in a hurry besides telling the people that instead of taking the halt time at the signal as wasted ,it should be used to reduce stress by taking breathing exercise (The Times of India dated 18/02/1998, 19/02/1998 and 20/02/1998). Moreover, at the glow of the red light , boldly written word 'RELAX' would welcome the people in the driving seats. The whole of Delhi was having this organized so well and it helped in a big way in controlling   traffic as well as bringing down the number of accidents in road mishaps.

13] Ministry of Science and Technology:

It comes up with beautiful print ads on May 11 every year which happens to be Technology day. Three ads on consecutive pages of The Times of India on 11/05/2002 explained the areas in which our country has made progress through effective use of technology viz., developing early, high yielding and genetically superior plant varieties or developing herbal cure for asthma or designing and producing a computer for illiterate or even having a satellite enabling accurate weather forecasts. The advertisements saluted the scientists, researchers and technologists who have done exceptionally well in order to take India to these heights. These ads generate a feeling of patriotism among all of us and at the same time make us resolve to improve further.

14] Citizens Vigilance Movement:

On 07/05/2002, this organization issued a beautiful print ad in The Times of India where 4 kids were shown totally ignorant of their surroundings and happy in their own little world. 'Ignorance is bliss' was the headline and the ad copy further explained the purity in the heart of a child. The ad space sponsored by makers of two leading brands of tea viz., Good Morning Tea and Tea Bags and Wagh Bakri tea clearly tried to drive down a message of purity and love during those troubled times of disturbances in Gujarat.

15] National Foundation for Communal Harmony:

This organization headquartered at New Delhi came up with a beautiful print advertisement at the height of communal riots in Gujarat (The Times of India dated 09/03/2002). The simple ad copy showed a child representing a riot affected kid sitting perplexed and the headline said

'What is religion?'. It further mentioned 'I don't even know my name!'. Only about ten words summed up the innocence of the child and also tried to convey to all who mattered at that time the urgency of stopping the riots as soon as possible.

16] Prathama Blood Centre:

This charitable trust based in Ahmedabad is an advanced transfusion medicine research foundation .It comes up with simple but well meaning print ads exhorting people to donate blood. On 24/02/2002, The Times of India showed its ad carrying a photo of a beautiful kid who happened to be haemophilic with the ad copy trying to convince the readers to save such lives by donating blood. At the time of communal riots in Ahmedabad, its ad in The Times of India dated 03/03/2002 carried statements like 'Blood is life, Let's not shed blood. Let's donate it to save life'. On the World Health Day(07/04/2002), it exhorted the readers to show there concern by donating blood(The Times of India dated 07/04/2002).

17] GlaxoSmithKline:

This organization advertised on a full page in The Times of India dated 19/01/2002 where it not only conveyed the message that most of the mothers in the world protect their children from a host of deadly diseases but they do so by getting them vaccinated GlaxoSmithkline(GSK) Vaccines. Although ,the ad clearly advertised vaccines but it also conveyed to all mothers that it is important that they get their children vaccinated at right times. The ad supported this aspect by giving statistical data related to vaccines all over the world.

18] Child Relief And You:

Popularly known as CRY, this Non Government Organization(NGO) is involved in carrying a lot of support activities for deprived Indian children by promoting and selling greeting cards, desk calendars, diaries, telephone and address books besides mini organizers through retail outlets on a regular basis. Its print ads are very touching. One particular ad which appeared in The Times of India dated 19/06/2001,26/11/2001 and 10/12/2001 carried lines 'A greeting card can make someone's day. A CRY card, someone's life.'

19] Amul:

This particular name is associated with so many advertisements for so many of its products but here it is important to mention one print ad which appeared in The Times of India dated 13/04/2002 . ' Caste. Community. Religion. Every morning in Gujarat, it all melts in a drop of milk. Milk accept all. Do you?' At the end of it ,it said 'Amul-The Taste of India'. At a time, when Gujarat was just limping back to normalcy from dark days of riots ,this advertisement was a real effort to apply language of reason to all right thinking people as well as people who were not ready to listen to voices of humanity.

20] The Indian Express:

This media vehicle has played a pioneering role in enlightening its readers about social causes, responsibilities, commitments towards mankind etc through its thought provoking advertisements from time to time. Although all such ads cannot be mentioned here, but still there is room for a few of them Since 1999, this media house is coming up with so thought provoking advertisements that anyone can get moved by them. It floated many print ads related to Adoption of a child with the base line *Adoption is one of the many social causes supported by the Indian Express*. One of the ad shows a child looking towards the reader with the headline saying *'Its not how you bring him into this world .Its how you bring him up'* In the same series of ads, one ad showed a lady holding a child with the headline saying *'I knew I could never have a baby.But I was still expecting one.'*

21] Maruti Udyog Ltd:

This famous brand in Indian automobile sector has not lagged behind in its commitment towards socially significant communications. Of the nine ads nominated in the Social Campaign category for London International Awards in 1998, two were from Maruti Udyog Ltd(MUL). These ads urged customers to obey traffic rules. Inanother ad, MUL picturized a familiar scene commonly seen in urban India i.e., talking on a cell phone while riding. The ad shows a man speeding through the traffic and talking on his cell to his girlfriend who has refused his proposal. Immersed in the conversation, he ignores the traffic signals: finally, she accepts his proposal but by that time he fails to see the truck coming in front of him. He utters his final words saying ' I can already hear the wedding bells ringing' and the spot ends with the cell phone on a bouquet of roses. By 2000 itself, Maruti commissioned around 36 short films as a part of its effort to develop socially relevant communication on topics like traffic rules and driving habits of people. It still carries on.

22] Escotel Mobile Communications Ltd:

Some advertisements from this service provider move the hearts of everyone.Aimed at promoting communal harmony, the company advertised prominently on Television during 2002 and is continuing it even during 2003. All its advertisements conveyed that the feeling of togetherness will benefit everyone if differences due to religion are not given prominence. With tagline 'Bringing People Closer' all the ads showed emotions at their best. If one ad showed Harbhajan Singh's mother praying for the success of Rahul Dravid, another ad showed Mohd Kaif's mother praying for the success of Sachin Tendulkar.In the same spirit, one another ad showed Virendra Sehwag's mother praying for the success of Zahir Khan. All the advertisements demonstrated the emotions which a mother carries for a child and for her, every child is like her son or daughter. Moreover, when the prestige of the country is involved whether it is a game of cricket or anything else, the heart of a mother becomes very large. So, why not learn these good things from one's mother or for that matter any mother in this world? These ads carry a strong meaning in an otherwise sharply divided society on the basis of religion and religious affiliations.

References

The Times of India	11/05/2002, 07/05/2002,16/04/2002, 13/04/2002, 07/04/2002,23/03/2002,09/03/2002,03/03/2002,24/02/2002, 26/01/2002,20/01/2002,19/01/2002,16/01/2002,10/12/2001,30/11/2001,26/11/2001,25/11/2001,07/11/2001,02/10/2001,01/10/2001,09/09/2001,08/09/2001,03/09/2001,02/09/2001,16/07/2001,11/07/2001,19/06/2001,18/06/2001,31/05/2001,30/05/2001,25/05/2001,24/05/2001,22/05/2001,20/02/1998,19/02/1998,18/02/1998
Indian Express	01/12/2001,25/06/2001,05/06/2001,25/05/2001,28/02/1998
The Hindustan Times	23/08/1998
India Today	29/02/1996

Company focus on Maruti, K Padma, Advertising Express Page 42-44

www.magindia.com

7. Socially Responsible Corporates: Reality or Misrepresentation

(This paper was presented at NIRMA INTERNATIONAL CONFERENCE ON MANAGEMENT (NICOM 2004) JANUARY 2-4, 2004 at Nirma Institute of Management, Sarkhej-Gandhinagar Hoghway, Post: Chandlodia, Via: Gota, Ahmedabad-382481,India). .

Corporate Social understanding:

"Besides being competitive, it is also imperative for the Indian industry to demonstrate corporate social responsibility. Becoming green and addressing environmental issues are steps towards this objective," *says Jamshyd N Godrej of the Godrej group*. "Many result-oriented organisations in India have initiated actions towards sustainability. They have in turn realised that investing in environmentally sound technologies reflects receptively in their balance sheets," *according to vice-chairman and chief executive officer of Dr Reddy's Laboratories*. "Collectively over 7,000 organisations, including Ford Motor, Apple Computers and 3M, are now partners for the environment and have led to an estimated annual cost savings of over $3.3 billion," *says Joan Fidler of US Environmental Protection Agency.*

These were views of some of the business leaders at the two-day first-ever Green Business Summit, which was held recently in Hyderabad. The summit ended up on a positive note with the corporate India vowing to go for green technologies and buildings in their quest for achieving sustainability and profitability.

The Big Six—the Tatas, the Birlas, the Godrej group, Reliance, ITC Limited and Dr Reddy's— have decided to go in for green buildings immediately to prompt others to follow. The Hyderabad summit not only increased awareness on green business concepts, but also highlighted the need to go in for green technologies to overcome the future challenges and competitiveness.

Concerned over their socio-environmental obligations, all participants deeply felt the urgency and the necessity of addressing these issues to improve the quality and bottom line of their organizations. These companies not only emphasized upon one another the importance of adopting green technologies, but also of addressing the issues of safety, health, environment and social obligations. The concept of globalization, deregulation, privatization and information technology have changed the perception of many corporates the world over towards their social responsibilities and Indian corporates too seem to be following the trend. Given the deliberations and discussions at the summit, it was obvious that many enterprises in India are at different stages on the path towards sustainable development. Some have started by addressing issues like pollution and safety, while others are adopting more strategic approach in addressing the society's economic, environmental and social concerns in an integrated manner. Many Indian companies also realized that investing in environmentally sound technologies can reflect profitably in their balance sheets. Many corporates did not even make much of the fact that the cleaner technology comes with an additional price tag.

"Adopting best practices in works significantly improves productivity and profitability and the Indian corporates, particularly Dr Reddy's, has realized that environmental sensitivity can help us grow more qualitatively than quantitatively by providing more services, functions and values rather than transforming more materials into energy and waste," *says Mr Prasad, who was also the chairman of Green Summit 2003.*

Green is competitive and sustainable. The point is driven home by Dr Reddy's recently introduced SHE (Safety, Healthy and Environment) performance report, Mr Prasad said at the inaugural session. Mr Godrej added that if one looks at the global scenario, the developed countries have already realized the adverse effects of unplanned growth and development—such as environmental pollution, toxic wastes, climate change, global warming, depletion of forest cover—and have accordingly invested heavily in green technologies. It holds lessons for developing countries like India. There is a need for us to have higher growth rates without "depriving future generations of natural resources and a healthy environment", Mr Godrej emphasized. At the two-day summit, the decision makers of the companies also deliberated upon the need to learn from the operation of ecosystem in nature, address the industrial ecology imbalances and adoption of best practices available in the world to improve productivity and profitability.

They also felt that the need of the hour is to adopt the principles of natural capitalism. Major issues like green building concepts, water treatment management, promoting waste recycling, practicing green concepts, desalination, incubating green businesses, harnessing renewable energy and conducting energy environmental audits were also discussed. During the two-day summit, the Confederation of Indian Industry also announced the launch of India's first Green Business Centre. It is being developed in collaboration with the Godrej group, Andhra Pradesh government and United States Agency of International Aid

Corporate Social Responsibility

Introduction: Corporate Social Responsibility(CSR) is a very hot topic in present scenario because it is not easy to evaluate. There are many variables like commitment to society, responsibility to stakeholders, labor, environment, education, customers. So it is critical to understand CSR.

Why companies are making a determined attempt towards CSR? Whether all the companies are (irrespective of their size and business)   fulfilling CSR? What it means to Indian companies? Before answering all the above questions and many more, first and foremost important thing is to understand CSR.

In the past, it was enough for a company to make a decent product and market it. These days, corporations should reach out to various stakeholders and win their confidence.

The objective of this deliberation is :

1) To understand Corporate Social Responsibility.

2) To understand Corporate Citizenship.

3) To understand variations existing in CSR regarding different industry sectors.

A small study in the city of Ahmedabad targeting Corporate Executives with a set of questions was undertaken and planned as follows:

Phase One

1) **Targeting Industrial Sectors**

- Management Consultancy

- Information Technology/ Software Development

- Finance

- Engineering

52

- Chemical Industry

- Construction Industry

- Power Generation

- Manufacturing

- Handicrafts/Textiles

- Service Industry

2) **Activities:**

- Taking appointments from concerned executives who were at the top level in management.

- Getting questionnaires filled by these people.

- To discuss beyond the questionnaire for getting personal views on CSR?

Other Questions*

- Is Company using CSR for getting fame?

- Is Company using CSR for making Brand value?

- Is Company using CSR for getting monetary benefits?

* These questions are used for getting real picture.

3) **Constraints**:

- Time Period

- Data available of targeted Industrial Sectors

Phase Two

Name of Companies approached:

- Xplora Design Skool.

- Adani Group

- Zydus Cadila

- Arvind Mills

- Ashima Group

Phase third

Analyses of data:

- About CSR, every respondent explained, "it is very important for any company and it would play a critical role in image building of the company." They avoided giving information of their policies adopted for CSR like Corporate Governance, Environment, Occupational Health and Safety, Education, Social Welfare, Anti-discrimination (womem/men, caste, religion, etc.), Community Development, Workers Rights/Child Labour, and Human Rights.

- They pointed out, " Corporate Social Responsibility is considered as critical variable, affecting   long term strategies ".So they think that Health and Safety, Social Welfare, Human Rights are important for survival of any company as today every information is available to everyone specially customers."

- The average rating of variables(on a scale of 1-10) are given below

Variables	Average Rating
Employers	7.5
Employees	9
Unions	5
Shareholders	7
Investors	8
Regulators(Govt. Authorities)	9
Community	8
Other/s like education, human right, social	6

- The average rating of attitude variables are given

Attitude Variables	Average Rating
Commercial Pressure	**9**
Rising international standards	8
Increasing awareness	7
Reputation	9
Public Opinion	7.5
Community group pressure	5
Rising domestic standards	9
Other/s like brand value	6.5

- Everybody said, "CSR is a need for any Indian company if it wants to achieve a dynamic culture like any multinational company. It is very important to understand the role of CSR in building a culture within the organization."

- They said that mostly companies adopted CSR because of improvement in long term strategies like image building etc.

- They pointed out following obstacles which Indian companies are facing

  ➢ Political problems

  ➢ Inefficiency of Indian Regulatory System

Other comments: they said, "Companies are using CSR as tools of promotion, advertising, getting awareness, image building, etc which bring non-monetary benefits to the companies. Sometimes they also get monetary benefits like spending money in social programs for avoiding taxes etc." So they said, "It is very difficult to define CSR in real words in corporate life."

Limitations of this analyses:

- It is based on a questionnaire, and responses could be biased, thereby projecting the company only in good light.

- Some personal interview can give incorrect information because respondents do not give importance to the real purpose of the interview.

Conclusion:

57

It can be very rightly said that Corporate Social Responsibility is catching up with Indian Corporates slowly and gradually.It does not matter whether the company is very big, big , small or very small. Although, this study targeted a small section of corporate fraternity in Ahmedabad and is not exhaustive, still it can be a good beginning of an elaborate and detailed further study.

Reference:

1. **The Times of India**

2. **The Indian Express**

3. **The Hindu**

4. **The Economic Times**

5. **Business Standard**

6. **Businessworld**

7. **Business Today**

8. Behavioral shift in consumers as a fall-out of socio-cultural dynamism

(This paper was presented by at Sixth National Conference on **"Enhancing Performance:Agenda for Growth"** January 30-31,2004 ,at **Prestige Institute of Management and Research** 2, Education & Health Sector, Scheme 54, Indore (M.P)-452010 INDIA)

Introduction: Behavior may or may not be related to any buying but it boils down to one's action towards buying any product or service. It also helps an individual to react in a way which again reflects the possibility of designing the marketing action on the part of the company/ies promoting their products and services. The conventional product life cycle is getting blurred now a days with very unpredictable nature of consumer responses towards all types of products. With mobility and connectivity becoming a part of life, mingling of cultural values play a significant role in modifying and re-modifying the behavior of consumers. Consequently, marketing strategies designed to attract such a volatile consumer also need to be modified and re-modified accordingly. Marketers are going to face the necessity of getting this type of study done regularly on any micro or macro level spread across different geographical locations depending upon the various constraints and avenues in which they are bound to operate. This paper throws light on these changes in consumer behavior which any company or marketing person would like to monitor with as much rapidity as possible. It also throws light on certain aspects which need not require any observation or monitoring. As part of the study conducted in Ahmedabad region, this paper goes straight away into the findings as to whether there is any behavioral shift in consumers or not and if it exists, is it due to socio-cultural dynamism or something else.

Methodology

Reading Factor Influences

➤ Sociocultural Influences: incorporate personal influences, reference groups, family influence, social class, and culture and subculture. An individual looks to these items with regards to following aspects

Personal: Assess other individuals opinions or behaviors in environment.

Reference groups: To measure self-worth or confirm beliefs.

Family influence: Decide needs based on stage in family life.

Social class: Check level of living with others in environment.

Culture and subculture: Check values, ideas, and attitudes in agreement with others in environment.

➤ Situational Influences deals with an individual's environment at the time of purchase including:

- purchase task - gift or need

- social surroundings - alone or in group

- physical surroundings - mall or boutique

- temporal effects - rushed or not rushed

- antecedent states - amount of money available

Survey Analysis

- Sample size of survey is 38

- Age and gender category division is shown in following table.

Age Group	Female	Male

Less then 25	17	3
Between 25-35	4	3
More then 35	10	1
Total – 38	31	7

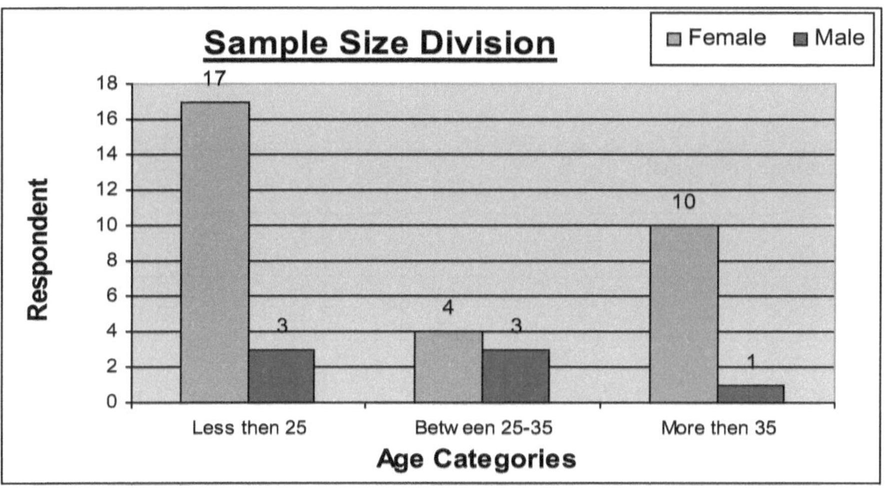

- Survey conducted on shifting of buying behavior among consumers affected by the culture and social group. Analysis of the survey is done on the basis of a questionnaire

  ➤ We asked the respondents about their buying behavior giving different options.

    The options are

    1) Very Meticulous,

    2) Meticulous,

    3) Neither Meticulous nor Casual,

    4) Casual

5) Very Casual

> Responses shown in following chart are

	Female	Male
Very Meticulous	9	0
Meticulous	11	2
Neither meticulous nor casual	8	0
Casual	2	4
Very Casual	1	1
Total – 38	31	7

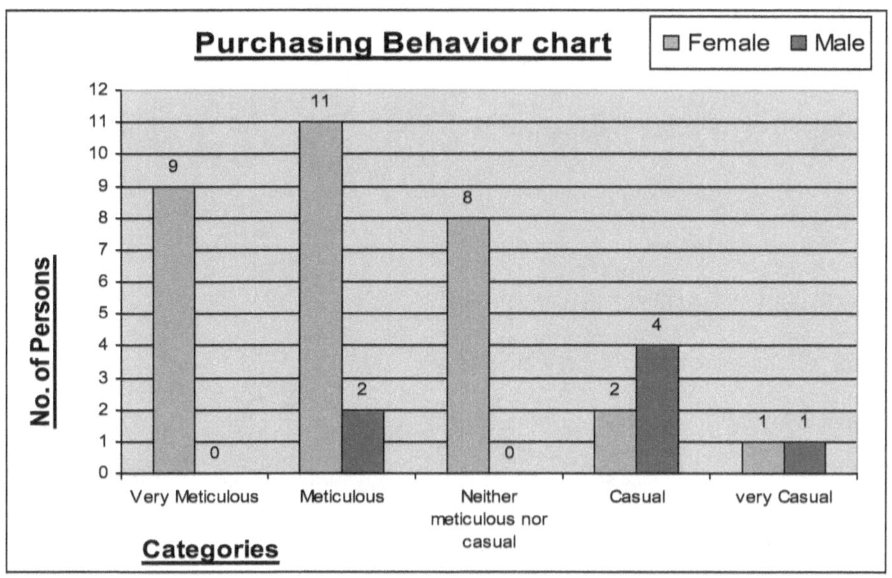

> In the first stage ,different reasons were given by respondents for selecting particular type of buying behavior. These reflect the changes taking place in the psyche of consumers   in the present environment. These reasons are :

For Very Meticulous buying behavior :

- Usually go for buying what is necessary and needed.

- After trying only once I can know the best.

- Want the best for myself .

- Want every thing that is premium.

- Have to look for the best for the family and it should suit them.

- Buy what I want.

- I know what suits me

- Tested and approved thing will be used.

For Meticulous buying behavior :

- No need to change until it works good and suits me.

- Faith on tried & tested brand presently using .

- Brands which I use are those upon which I trust.

- I'm brand loyal.

- Since long I live in a hostel so, what ever is under my budget I can go for it but of good quality.

- Things needed for family must be purchased.

- Go for quality product.

- Why should I look for other options if I am satisfied with the existing one

- I do not change the brand.

- Most of the things are repeat and I don't want to experiment.

- Things required by the family must be purchased.

- What ever I am using suits me so no point of change.

- Decision taken by mother.

For neither meticulous nor casual :

- Just for the sake of buying.

- Some brand do not change where as some get innovated almost every month.

- Don't want to waste time to think and I just take it out from display shelf.

- I should use the option to choose the best for me.

- I'm neither too focused nor too casual about key duties.

- I know what suits me.

- I like to live free without any interference.

- Decision taken by mother.

For casual buying behavior

- Depends on market availability.

- Feel like trying every thing.

- I believe in taking life as it comes naturally.

- Not interested in buying things.

- Not interested to go for a particular brand

- It basically depends on my mood

For very casual buying behavior

- Like to change brand on every purchase.

- I don't bother about any thing and just purchase, use and feel it.

➢ In second stage of questionnaire we asked the consumers whether their buying behavior gets affected by social groups or not.

- *14 respondent said that social group does not affect their buying behavior.* They give different reasons like:

  - Why should I follow others.

  - I have my own style.

  - Why should I copy others

  - I don't interfere in other's situations.

  - We choose by ourselves what we like, I don't care about the society.

- Its our choice and interest, not the society's..

- Why should I change for others.

- I know what I need and what suits me.

- *5 respondents said that sometimes social groups affect.*

  They give reasons like

- Sometime change in social atmosphere is good so I adopt it.

- Certainly when people around me suggest that something would look nice on me, I

  buy that product.

- Often if someone tell that particular product is fine then I go for it.

- Sometime , friends advise to buy a [product because of performance level of the

product.

- Not always but for some good products.

- *19 respondents accepted the affect of social group on their buying behavior.*

- It depends upon the opinion of friend, family.

- Some influence is always their when u r in society as a whole.

- New innovations are to be welcomed.

- Good things are to be accepted.

- Friends have an influence on me.

- I am a social being.

- Change as per society trends.

- Friends play a major role in my decisions.

- Friends and elder people influence me.

- Want to be in trend.

- If some thing is new and it looks good, it should be accepted.

- I want to be with the trend.

- As a matter of fact society affects any decision.

- What ever is good is accepted.

- I should have what ever is in my affordability limit .

- Social factors can be effective.

- Any good things are to be accepted.

- I used to be a high price brand user.

➢ By following the stage further we asked the consumers whether the culture plays any important role in their buying behavior.

- *14 respondents accept that culture does affect their buying decision .*

    The reasons given by them are :

    - Yes because I am an Indian and north Indian.

    - Yes as I do product selection up by analyzing its composition , I prefer mostly herbal products.

    - Its very difficult to be away from our roots, so some effect will be there.

    - Yes what ever I feel like buying is subjected to over all family attitude.

    - Yes shopping is done by family members. I just use what they buy

    - Yes some times but generally not.

    - Yes usually use things available in my home.

    - Yes some impact is always their because we live as family and decide as a whole.

    - To a certain extent but not in a big way as my parents have given me the freedom.

    - Yes I'll not go beyond my limit.

- Joint family hence it has effect on every family member .

- Yes , brands remain constant.

- Yes, because I believe that I am also a consumer who has many choices.

- Yes, family has an important place.

- Yes, family is must.

- Culture has to be followed and respected.

- Yes, family behavior provide us with guideline.

- *24 respondents said that to some extent culture plays an important role in their buying behavior.*

   The reasons given by them are:

- No specific culture followed by us

- No, I am free to choose what ever is good for me but within the parameter of the family.

- No restriction from the home and family.

- No we are free to new ideas.

- No, every body is free to make his her own choice.

- No,   I don't bother about it.

- No, there is no restriction from my home.

- No, I believe in integration of culture .

- No, as I'm living out of my home for more than 7 year now.

- No, I decide my own parameters.

- No restriction from the home.

- I'm free to purchase what ever I needed but have to take care of others sentiments.

- May be or may not be, it depends on interaction.

➢ Following the questionnaire, we asked the consumers for their preferred brand in different categories of products like :

- o Hair Oil
- o Shampoo
- o Cream – Cold, Vanishing
- o Moisturizer
- o Talcum powder
- o Tooth paste
- o Bathing soap

- Some preferred brands for Hair Oil are :

  Keo Karpin, Vatika, Himalaya, Hair care, Parachute, Navratan, shiny, All Clear, Ayush, Bajaj Almond, Clinic Plus, Dabur Amla, Banphool, Ayur, Marico

- Some preferred brands for Shampoos are: :

  Garnier, Heads & Shoulders , Sun Silk, Clinic Plus, Pantene , Vatika, Shehnaz Hussain, L'oreal , Hello, Madhuri, Nile, Ayur.

- Some preferred brands for Fairness Cream are:

  Ponds, Fair & Lovely, Nivea, L'oreal , Garnier, Shehnaz Hussain, Lakme

- Some preferred brands for Cold Cream are:

Lakme, Nivea, Ponds, L'oreal, Vasline, Shehnaz Hussain, Ayur

- Some preferred brands for Vanishing Cream are:

  Lakme, Nivea, Ponds, L'oreal, Fair & lovely

- Some preferred brands for Moisturizer are :

  Ponds, Lakme, Vasline, Lotus, Garnier, , L'oreal

- Some preferred brands for Talcum Powder are :

  Liril, Denim, She, Fa, Ponds magic, Nycil

- Some preferred brands for Tooth Paste :

  Colgate, Pepsodent, Forhans, Dabur lal, Neem, Closeup

- Some preferred brands for Bathing Soap :

  Mysoor Sandal, Liril, Lux, Santoor, Dettol, Dove, Neema, Pears, Cinthol, Breeze, Life buoy- gold, Hamam, Santoor, Nivea.

Results and Discussion (Conclusion) :

- As per the survey, today consumers are more conscious in choosing and selecting particular brand in any particular product category.

- While they don't directly accept the social and cultural affect on their buying behavior but reflection of socio-cultural is there to see in their use of preferred brands in a particular product category.

- Today consumers are applying different mindsets. If they are satisfied with a brand of particular product, they become loyal to that brand and do not to prefer to shift or try to move to other brand.

- In present scenario preference to herbal and quality products is increased and importance is attached to a special feature of the product like under hair oil categories, importance to herbal and non sticky oil is greater.

- In shampoo, anti dandruff and conditioning with good quality products are on top of the list. Price does not make any difference in buying behavior of shampoo.

- In fairness cream, with different categories like cold and vanishing cream, consumers mostly prefer good quality, trusted, suited to there body with special benefits like protection of skin from sunlight, increase in face shine, removal of pimples from face etc . Price doesn't make any difference in buying. Some consumers also give preference to fragrance of the cream.

- In Talcum Powder, fragrance is the main feature in selecting brand. Different consumers have different tastes which affect the brand decision.

- In Tooth Paste, trust and protection from germs are main features in selecting a particular tooth paste brand.

- Bathing Soap is such a category in which variance of preferred brands is very high. Importance is given by the consumer to that brand which gives him a feeling of freshness for a long time.

- Finally, society and culture play an important role in buying behavior. Whether they accept it openly or not but influences do take place directly or indirectly affecting their buying decisions in day to day life. Sociocultural Influcences: take place by personal contacts , reference groups, family, social class, and culture and subculture. Situational Influences deal with an individual's environment at the time of purchase which also comes to light in this survey e.g., a mother selecting one best brand baby soap for her new born baby which takes care of his health and protects him from germs.

9. Market sensing : The contemporary way

(This paper was presented at 'National Conference On Marketing 2004 and Beyond' organized by ICFAI Business School, Bangalore, India during Oct 28-29,2004).

Sensing the market is a very sensible thing to do for any business scenario. Gone are the days when a company making any product can think of some times or phases where it can monopolize the situation/s. Even the word competition appears to be very simple. Almost every company making all types of products or providing any type of service accepts the presence of competition to its existence. A smart company is that which respects the competition and never takes it lightly .A smarter company goes slightly beyond that where it anticipates the moves of its challengers, big or small and proactively handles the situation. The fact is that the number of such smarter companies are many and every one of them is out to prove itself better than the other. Over and above these two types of companies are those organizations which take lead and force others to compete in order to remain in the market. These are the organizations which lead from the front in whichever business they are and make sure that the competition is always following them. These are the companies which are actually sensing the market and making sure that they always remain ahead. This makes them continuosly on the top or only go down . That situation enhances their responsibility towards their public (customers, distribution, suppliers, regulators as well as competitors etc). These market sensing companies are held in high esteem by all their public and their publics at times swear by them. The activities which these companies do appear common and form the bedrock of marketing but the way in which they do them differentiates them from those companies which are below them in business hierarchy. These activities are as follows:

a. **Re-inventing core concepts of marketing**: All the companies are aware that starting from needs and passing through wants , desire, demand and all the way to product, market, satisfaction and value, marketing makes use of these words to suit its purpose. Product and companies may vary but concepts remain the same. Smartest companies have always found latent needs within consumers and always capitalized on them. Others then followed and joined the race. One can take the example of Maruti Udyog ltd which pioneered the concept of small cars in India and worked on the quality and numbers of roads in India(rural as well as urban sector). Off-course, there are so many examples of other brands which have found out some important inputs from the market which have made an outrageous idea successful in the long run. In the recent past which can be traced to late 1990s and early 2000s, a company like Hyundai designed and promoted a car which was positioned as a car for working women in the driver's seat and comfortable in a saree. Now here, working women and their numbers have always existed and will continue to increase, but the need of such women to put on a native attire even when working gets highlighted and that too from a company which is not much known for its association with saree. How many working women have taken it seriously and how many of them got influenced by it is a different matter.

b. **Shackling the environment of marketing;** As a matter of fact, what appeared to be environmental barriers in the past have become environmental assets for the marketers. A very good and long list of companies can be unearthed within India which ascribe to this viewpoint. In a state like Gujarat where liquor consumption is banned due to it being a dry state, consumption of other drinks has always remained high and marketers for such drinks have taken full advantage of this ban. Moreover, people from Gujarat having a fancy for hard drinks can always go to neighboring Daman and Diu or even to Maharashtra regularly, have their take and come back. In fact, distributors and retailers of liquor brands in these parts of India have ensured that requirements of people coming from Gujarat is always met and they don't feel deprived of their take when they come for this purpose only. Then surrogate advertising for liquor brands has given a very cool way to their sponsors to air their names attached with a common product whereas actually the name implies a liquor brand thereby enhancing the recall to the viewer or listener. It would have been unheard till even mid 80s but later on it developed like a wild fire because marketers of liquor realized that consumers of their products will like to have such campaigns on TV even if it is done in a surrogate manner.

c. **De-mystifying consumer behavior and its study**; Consumer behavior and its study has become very dynamic because consumer itself has become very dynamic. The reasons for it can be found in tremendous travel which an individual does in the present times as well as intellectual travel which one does in the form of very rapid thinking in every area. These dynamisms have become very prevelant inspite of a revolution in connectivity through internet which lessens the reasons for physical travel. If we look at this whole phenomena in a holistic manner, the basis of studying consumer behavior will also become very volatile. We go into the cultural, social, psychological aspects etc of consumer behavior in its dynamism and try to reach to a conclusion. This helps us in formulating as well as re-formulating marketing strategies from time to time. But, due to the above reasons, this measurement also becomes outdated after regular intervals and it needs to be measured again and again. Companies know very well that every such exercise takes a lot of time, money etc and when its frequency increases, this cost also increases But every company knows very well that such types of studies are unavoidable That makes companies to have people within as well out of its ranks who can sense such trends etc at times and organized consumer behavior study not resorted to always.

d. **Upgrading Segmenting, Targeting and Positioning;** Segmenting, Targeting and Positioning, commonly known as STP is a very important exercise which needs to be continuously upgraded with times. This means that the concepts and foundations will remain the same and the application part will vary according to the situations. Marketers need to be dynamic in understanding these varying situations and apply STP accordingly. An example can be market segmentation for refrigerators during season and during off-season. A smart marketer should be well aware of the fact that when so-called summer season is not there, a refrigerator can be highlighted as a very strong consumer durable which doubles up as food preserving device. Food preservation characteristic is always there in a refrigerator but during summers the marketing communication pitch hovers around using it as a coolant in the form of cold drinks, beverages, and ice-creams etc. Many times, it is seen that marketers promote refrigerators only through sales promotion during off-season. There can be numerous examples where differentiated STP at different points of time will make marketers and their products (seasonal or non-seasonal) go well with the market. But , all involved in marketing have to be constantly vigilant and agile like a hawk in order to read from anywhere be it air, road or even from nowhere. It is because one does not know from where an idea can come and in which direction it can

get lost.

e. **Playing havoc with product development**: Many times, it so happens that in the name

of product development companies do a blunder which lands an otherwise good march of

the company into a disaster. Those who support the so called product development call it

a great idea but they fail to realize that unless the requsite volume of market does not

exist an idea should not be put into commercialization. On the other hand, it is better to

wait after reaching the stage of launch if market sensing tells that the proposed product

would be ahead of its times At times, the market is found already clutered with a similar

type of products and there is no use of adding one more with no any major difference in

features, attributes or performance standards. This concept is applicable to all types of

industries viz., automobile, fast moving consumer goods, service sector,

etc. It so happens that although the idea is very good but the time is not right.At such

times, organizations requires market sensors in the form of continuously research

oriented teams guided by able and capable heads who are always ready with the right

sense of the market through every angle. Moreover, all involved with product

development require to respect the opinion and word of such people in organizations.

f. **Pricing used as a dynamic tool**: Every company uses this important P of marketing in

order to make market sensing more interesting .By deliberately playing with the price, a

company tries to gauge the mood of the target audience in the form of their reaction

patterns towards the quality of the product, the service offered along with the product etc.

In India, it is the normal behavior of consumers to start suspecting quality or feature reduction once the price reduction takes place. Normally consumers do not relate to less costing to the company or improved cost-volume ratio thereby making the product available to end users at reduced prices. As a result of this, many companies run campaigns to educate the users as well as potential users to make them aware of the reasons for such price cuts. On the other hand, an increase in price is normally related to better quality and additional features by maximum consumers. Naturally, companies welcome such a perception. In this whole exercise which involves all tools of marketing, market sensing in the form of consumer insights and their perceptions come to the fore. The more the company is professional, the better is the quality of the response, whether it is done by company employees or done by some outside agency. This whole exercise helps in identifying loop-holes as well as strong points in pricing strategies.

g. **Making promotion defy logic at times:** Many times, it appears that the way promotion is done is very illogical. But , actually speaking, whichever tool is used to promote different types of products , promotion is done keeping in mind the sensibility of the market. If we look at the TV advertisement of Intel Pentium chip, it looks ridiculous ,but it is this speed and productivity which is expected from it.This expectation of its users and potential users forces its promoters to advertise it in this way.When a newspaper ties up with a glass ware company or any other company making daily use items and brings out coupons in its edition which can be redeemed by readers at select outlets for certain gift items, it amounts to promotion.This promotion serves dual purpose of making the newspaper more open to its readers who buy more copies and at the same time glass ware company supplies more to the newspaper organization for its distribution.The outlet where coupons get redeemed also gets some benefit from both organizations besides getting publicity The reader gets a good gift at the end through coupon redemption. We can see the way in which a single day promotion brings benefit to a number of important constituents in a delivery chain. Many people who go by convention scoff at all this but then the numbers queuing up at such jamborees are not insignificant and just can't be ignored by all involved in marketing and creating brand awareness and recall.

h. **Re-inventing distribution network**: The distribution networks have existed and will continue to exist for products of all types. What is different in the present times is the way in which these have got re-invented by the constituents themselves. Instead of behaving as separate entities tied up loosely, these constituents actually work together so that frictions at any link points do not emerge at all. The reason behind all this is that end user at the retail point is not going to listen to any argument about delay on the part of the wholesaler or distributor for the non-availability of the product on the shelf. More important is the fact that this realization has come on the distribution network members on their own and without any pressure or force. Many companies in various sectors have formed an association which incorporates supply chain on one side and distribution network on the other side with the company in between and the whole chain working in total coordination so that the last link i.e., end user is troubled the least. The company has made this association more closer to every one within and outside the company by putting it on the website and facilitating Business to Business(B2B) as well as Business to Consumer(B2C) transactions as comfortable as possible.

i. **Making ethics very subjective:** The word ethics has acquired lot of relevance and significance due to marketing and that too in the recent past. In order to sense markets, marketers resort to certain practices which become topics of debate related to ethics, Most of the times ethics relate to confusing language used in marketing communication which lead to controversies between the consumer and the retailer at times. At certain other times, sex and its covert display in advertisements lead to issues which acquire ethical dimensions. Due to cultural and social differences between geographical areas where products/services are marketed, such issues get noticed fast and make the companies liable to be subjected to ethical criticism. After much damage has already been done, rectifications are applied and the marketers try to salvage the situation. These developments have highlighted the need for market sensing from the point of view of cultural and social sensitivities which vary from market to market. Although companies do give importance to these aspects but sometimes either due to indifference or due to some hidden realities, these problems crop up and market sensing is found wanting. It is true that nothing can be full proof in this world and same goes for market sensing but as far as possible, ethical dilemmas can be avoided by keeping in touch with the market at all times and giving importance to these touch points.

References:

1. Pg 42 ,Marketing Mastermind, July 2001.

2. Pg 10 , Businessworld   19-03-2001

3. Pg 24 , Businessworld   19-02-2001.

4. 'Scene from the Malls', Business India , 13-26 Nov,2000.

5. Asitava Sen, 'The Channel Challenge' , Business Standard, Oct 17, 2000.

6   'Banking in Retail Raj', Aruna Vaidyanathan , The Economic Times, Jan

    12,2000 and Marketing Mastermind, July 2001, Pages 48-49.

7   Modern Retailing in India', Sanchita Das, Business India, November 13-26,

    2000 and Marketing Mastermind, July 2001, Pages 50-53.

8   'The Price of Loyalty', James Cigliano, Margaret Georgiadis, Darren Pleasance

    , Susan Whalley , www.mckinseyquarterly.com and Marketing Mastermind,

    August 2001, Pages 14-19.

9   ' Shoppers won't stop-But Indian Retailing is at Crossroads', G.D.Singh,

    www.indiareacts.com, Dec 12,2000 and Marketing Mastermind, August 2001,

    Pages 41- 43.

10 The Retailing Road Map', Priya Chandrasekhar, Business Line,Catalyst,

    February 15,2001 and Marketing Mastermind, September 2001 Pages 28-31.

11 Finding the right Retail Model', Shreenivasa Chakravarti, Business

    Line,Catalyst, February 22,2001 and Marketing Mastermind, September 2001

    Pages 32-34.

12 'Creating Customer and Shareholder value in Retail Marketplace' summarized

version of the White Paper   " Creating Customer and Shareholder Value in Retail Marketplace" by Accenture and Marketing Mastermind December 2001 Pages 20-21.

13 Business Intelligence and Retailing', Srinavasa Rao P, Saurabh Swarup, www.wipro.com and Marketing Mastermind, April 2002 Pages 60-65.

14 White Goods on Solo Run', Mayanka M Singh, Businessworld, August 5,2002 Pages 52-54

15 'Adopt a service mindset', Case study by Meera Seth, Busuinessworld, January 13,2003, Pages 45-48

16 'Conflict Street', M Rajshekhar, Businessworld, March 24,2003, Pages 36-37

10. Tour Operators Marketing Efforts to Meet Honeymooners Expectations

(This paper was presented at Second AIMS International Conference On Management (AIMSiCOM2) on "Managing in a Global Economy: Emerging Challenges to Management Profession" December 28-31, 2004 at Indian Institute of Management, Kolkata, India)

The aspect of marriage will always be a very potential source of business for tour and travel operators interested in exploiting the market of honeymoon travel. Although marriage is a very social activity which involves some sensitive understanding as India is a diverse country with numerous cultural leanings. Tour operators may not like to go into all this while offering their packages, but they can definitely harp on certain commonalities across all cultures and social classes. These commonalities can be the uniqueness of honeymoon in all social and religious groups, the degree of affluence which has come up across all classes, the common expectations of all classes while going on honeymoon and the care and hospitality expected by these people wherever they go on such a special trip.In the details described, the word honeymooners imply couples who went on their honeymoons immediately after marriage.

Globalization: This word has caught fancy of many Indians ever since Indian market opened to outsiders and companies from abroad found it feasible to build, develop and sustain business in India. This has brought the scope of traveling to and from India enlarge and acquire very high proportions. Here we will concentrate on outbound tour and travel with special reference to honeymoon traveler from Ahmedabad. One very prudent thinking in this direction is that it is this age of people who like to take risks and explore as they will not be getting the same quality time to enjoy at any time in future. Globalization has encouraged the risk taking abilities of such highly talented and pleasure-seeking individuals. Moreover, in Ahmedabad, which happens to be a very happening city as far as enterprising minds are concerned, the coming together of pleasure trip i.e., honeymoon and business travel has always worked. At the same time, the wooing of this category of traveler by tour operators has incorporated this dual purpose while on a journey. In a sample of 100 honeymooners (couples) surveyed during April-June 2004, the impact of Globalization was felt in the following manner

Type of impact	No of couples
Weak	23
Mild	28
Strong	49

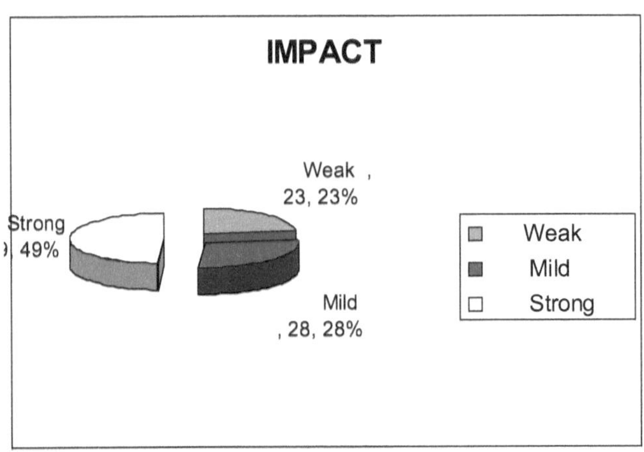

The figures given above hint at simple numbers but these have a definite meaning. Weak and mild combine to make 51% respondents which might hint that half of the sample population is almost ineffective to the impact of globalization. But on the other hand 49% strong figure hint in the direction that the phenomena of globalization has taken many young couples to the desire of high places. The reasons attributed by this category of respondents are

1. Overlapping/combining business visits with leisure trips

2. General attitude of welcome for Indians present at all destinations

3. Over-all image of India getting improved across the world as a country of intellectuals, ,hard-working and needing a qualitative break from work

Spiraling salaries: It is a common phenomenon in India that salaries in private sector for junior and middle level of employees have become very high and this helps young couples in there mid and late 20s plan their honeymoons in the most organized manner. The simple fact is that in eighties and even in nineties, honeymoon plans got curtailed or drastically overhauled due to monetary considerations which is not the case now. In a city like Ahmedabad, where young aspiring entrepreneurs as well as service class executives live in gay abundance, disposable money has never been a problem. Moreover, with an activity which is to take place once in a lifetime should not be cut short or dove tailed on monetary grounds. Out of 100 couples surveyed, the response pattern can be distributed as follows

Reasons	*No of couples*
# Life is too short, enjoy now	74
# Who knows when this abundance of money will end	11
# Once responsibilities increase, time for such travels will never be there	11
# No specific reasons in mind	04

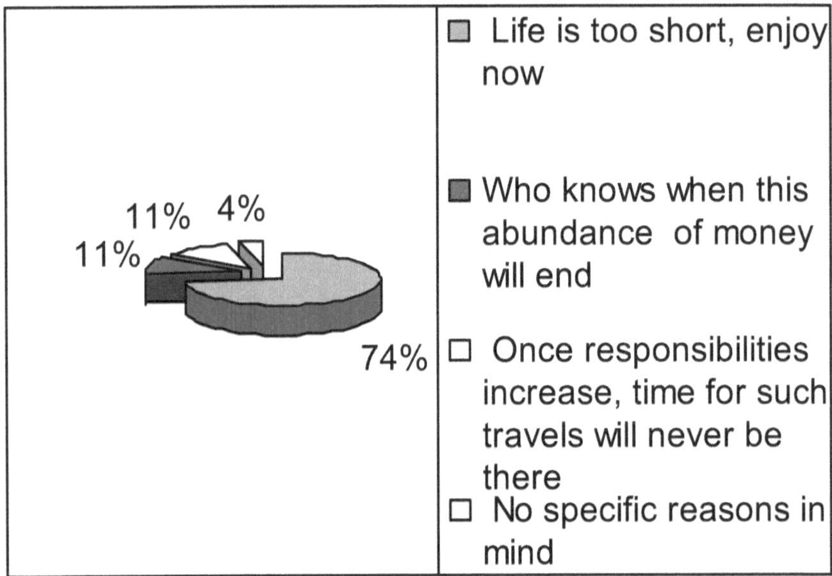

Easy access to internet: Internet has made a lot of information and its availability very easy and at ones convenience. Honeymooners have the comfort of identifying their type of vacation, destinations, adventure spots etc available at the click of the mouse where the websites of various travel and tour operators have contributed in this activity actively. Moreover, the internet is also aiding the handling of existing and potential customers at the office when actual negotiations start to finalize the tour. Internet at home, office or even in the form of cybercafes in Ahmedabad has made the task of interested couples as well as the tour operators more fast and result oriented. The 100 couples participating in this study felt in various ways related to internet

Factor related to internet	No of couples
User friendly website of Tour operator	56
Tour operator website as pop-up available everywhere of the internet	24
Complete solutions from the tour operator available on internet	10

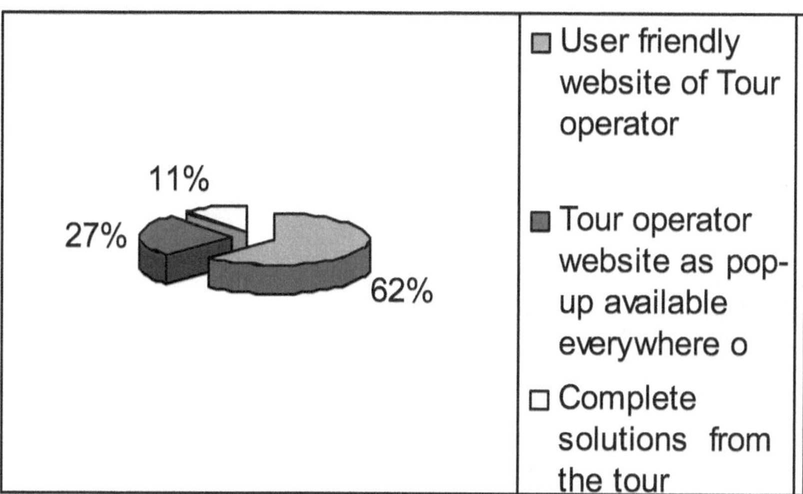

Ready availability of travel loans: Banks in private sectors as well as other lending agencies have come forward providing loans for travel and tours which can be re-payed in easy monthly installments later on. Apart from banks , it is the tour operators which are providing such a facility to their patrons thereby making travel enjoyable and free of any tensions. *We have to make it clear here that these loans are mostly offered by tour and travel organizers/agencies and not any bank etc.*The sample respondents totaling 100 gave following varied reasons for taking loans and going on tours

Reason for taking loans	No of couples
Affordable EMIs	57
Disposable income favors it	23
Spending whole amount in one go	
Is unimaginable	14
When everything can be enjoyed on loan,	06
why can't traveling be done	

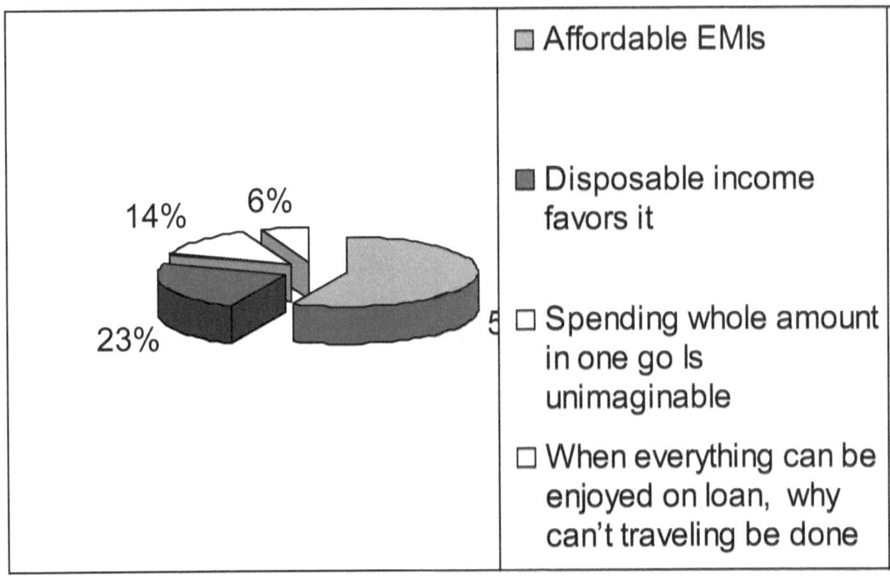

Late marriages; Marriages are usually said to be made in heavens. It is true but at times, these are also made on earth. We mean to say that unless and until a reasonably fair degree of financial stability is not perceived by the two persons interested, they do not marry. This results in some time getting consumed but for the people involved it is not wastage of time but in-fact investment of time. According to such couples, marrying at 30 or even beyond that is not late and they can plan to go anywhere as the basis of their so called late marriage i.e., financial stability will take care of all expenses. In my sample of 100 honeymooning couples 48 were in the category of late marriages i.e.s age group of 30 plus (husband as well as wife), following various reasons were given for late marriages

Reasons for late marriages	No of couples
Reaching a fair degree of financial stability	18

Compatable life-partner search took

Time   19

Family matters delayed marriage   11

                 Total   48

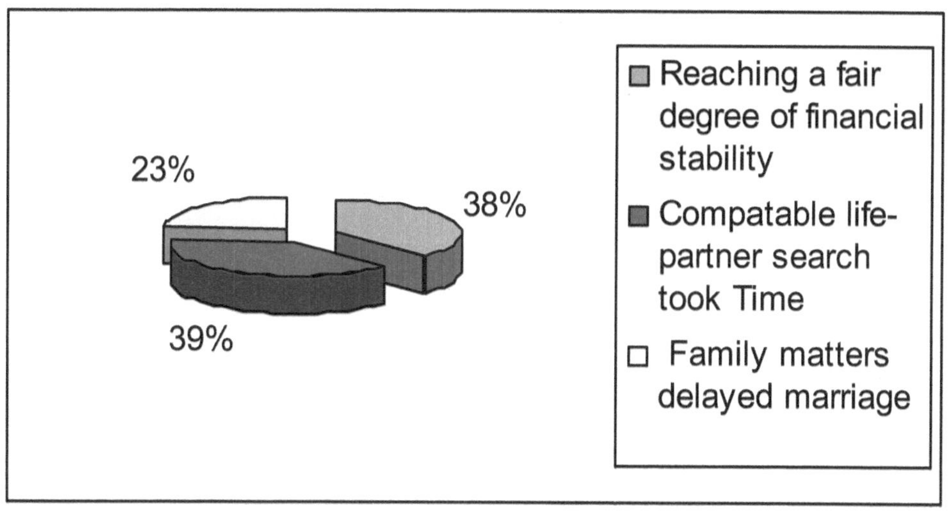

Double-income couples: In the present times, youngsters have a number of desires and interests for various things in life in a short span of time, This drives them much before marriage either on their own or through mutual understandimg, to work and generate money with the objective of planning for near as well as distant future. So whether it is man and woman knowing one another and going to have love marriage or they are not knowing one another and going to have an arranged marriage, both of them work and expect their would be spouse to be working respectably. Such double income couples are increasing and these are encouraging others to fall in their category. Ultimately it brings more money into the house and spends can become varied depending upon their tastes. It get very well reflected in the honeymoon aspect which happens to be the first organized outing in their new life. Due to its uniqueness, they are open to spend lavishly on it. In my study, all couples happened to be double income and that helped the tour operators market their offerings with a fair degree of comfort. The reasons cited by these 100 couples to be double income are as follows:

Reasons for double income	No of couples
More disposable money available	57
A fair degree of respect for one another	23
Crisis in one's job can be offset by other's job	11
A right future for kids to come later on	09

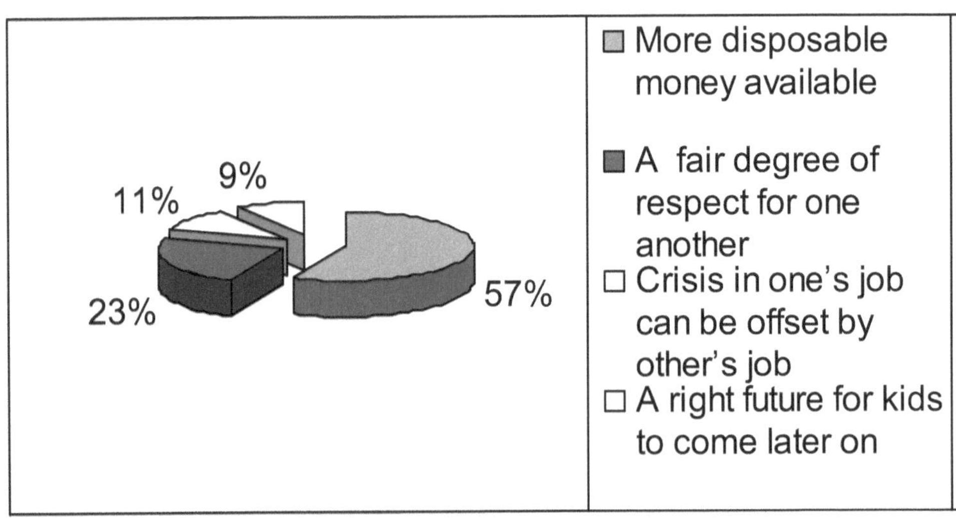

Conclusion: From the above discussion following things can be inferred and which can form a basis for detailed research either in more numbers or in a widespread geographical area or a combination of both.

a. Impact of Globalization has made it presence felt and Indian honeymoon traveler has matured to it.

b A big majority(more than 70 %) of Indian honeymooners are enjoying and interested to continuously enjoy the boom in their salaries and not much worried about savings in big way

c A host of solutions through the internet has made tour operators come very closer to honeymooners and it helps in minimizing problems

d Easy availability of travel loans has made the task of honeymoon travel less worrisome and more enjoyable. More than half of honeymooners have felt that when most of their household items of luxury are aquired through loan repayments, then there is no harm in repaying for honeymoon travel.

e. Marrying late (i.e., both in 30 plus age bracket) makes their financial planning better and disposable income more to experiment with. But this segment of honeymooners need to be researched more.

f. Double income couples feel more comfortable in trying out lavish honeymoons and they have no qualms about it. More than 50 percent of such couples are open to lavish honeymoons as this is a one time affair which should be enjoyed with full vigor.

Reference:

1. " Travel Induatry's date with honeymooners" , The Times of India-Ahmedabad dated: March 11, 2004

2. " The Brand that is India", Case study by Meera Seth, Businesworld dated June 16, 2003 Pg 30 -37

3. " Konkan Railway:The Sky is no limit" , T Surender, Businesworld dated March 25, 2004 Pg 30 -34

4. " India makes big at Cannes Ad Festival", Advertising Express, August 2003, Pg 11-13

5. " Pop Psychology", Debbie MacInnis,Advertising Express, December 2001, Pg 31-35

6. " Customer Service: Owning the relationship", Marketing Mastermind, July 2001

7. www.traveljini.com

8. www.startravelasia.com

9. www.goodwindtravels.com

10. www.thomascook.co.in

11. www.orbit-world.com

12. www.planmyholiays.com

13. www.palaceonwheelsindia.com

14. www.rajasthantourismindia.com

15. www.**sotc**tours.com

16. www.**cox**and**kings**.com

11. Customer-Satisfaction to Delight

(This Paper was presented at Sixth International Conference on Operations and Quantitative Management on the Theme 'Intelligent Decision Making: Emerging Strategy for Global Winners' during August 9-11, 2005 at Indian Institute of Management, Indore, MP, India)

It's a sad statement, but today's customers have come to expect adequate or, in some instances, less than adequate service from the organizations with which they come in contact. Customers do <u>not</u> expect to have their needs routinely anticipated and surpassed . . . to be genuinely impressed by the quality of personalized service . . . in short, to be *delighted* by their customer experience. But at the same time, customers can be expected to come out gradually or even radically with new desires, features and characteristics in their preferred products and brands. It helps organizations to keep these potential and latent expectations continuously under a scanner and adapt according to times as far as possible. At times, it is also required to make supposedly impossible things possible.

Customer Delight is the process of ensuring that every customer interaction consistently demonstrates organization's commitment to exceeding customer expectations. Customer Delight goes well beyond customer satisfaction. When practiced at all levels, it sets an organization on a different trajectory from the crowd and positions it as the organization of choice for current and potential customers. Customer Delight has to become a core value of the organization. It can happen only when those involved in every aspect of the business become active contributors to the process.

It is often said that marketers have to work towards customer delight through customer satisfaction. But, this very premise needs to be corrected. In fact, the whole organization needs to have a focus towards customer delight and it just can't be left to the marketing department. I'm sure that organizations which continuously encourage inculcating and promoting a culture within themselves where customer satisfaction to delight path principle pervades each and every individual and department,are the organizations which remain successful. Following diagram shows the aspects which go into making customer delight possible.

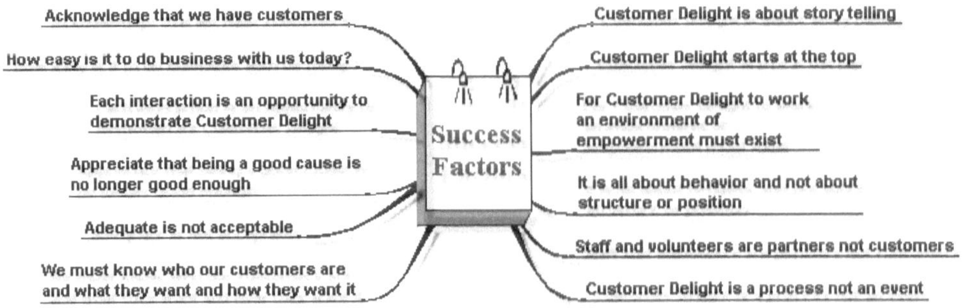

We will go into each and every aspect in some detail.

1. **Keep on acknowledging to customers about their valued existence** : It is very important to continuously communicate with customers and thanking them for their regular patronage. This involves all the stages of Supply Chain in one direction as well as Distribution Channel members in the other direction right up to the end user. What is more important is to keep on looking for feedbacks from the customers It so happens that when customers find themselves important in the company's activity

profile, they feel good about the company and ***spread a positive word of mouth***. At some point of time or other, this positive word of mouth does get translated into business. When Maruti came up with *Swift*, it tried to do exactly that through various media vehicles. All its communications portrayed that customers and their valued existence is very much behind the development of the model and the company looks forward to their feedback in future. The company conveyed the message of rich car which goes beyond the established perception of a normal car.It also made it look rich by highlighting space, refined outlook and user-friendliness besides elegant designing both outside as well as inside the car. In fact, by doing so it brought to -gether European styling, Japanese precision and Global appeal which it highlighted well.

2 **How easy is it to do business with us today**: In the present times, when competition knows no limit, it becomes significant for the company to explain the reasonability as well as compatibility of doing business with it to all its patrons viz., suppliers, distribution network as well as end-users. Now, it all appears very easy to say. But, then, it has to be done in any case. Whether the motive is to delight the customer by creating a new market or move the customer from satisfaction to delight in the existing market, the message of delight has to be put across in the simplest form through the most easily understandable vehicle of communication. Off-course, the company has to ensure that it does not overdo anything. A famous company which continues doing all this to make customer interface cool at every stage is LML

Limited. This in turn delights its audience. LML can be credited with so many firsts viz., metallic colors in 2 wheelers, brand retail outlets (LML World), electronics in scooters, single seat in scooters in India - this was not just a styling feature but made riding on scooters both for the driver and the pillion rider more comfortable than it had ever been before. Other firsts included 4 S motorcycles with more than two valves, celebrity endorsement where , in 1992, Kapil Dev successfully endorsed the LML Select brand of scooters, offer two dozen colour variants on one product{motorcycle), two wheeler Company to be authorised to issue vehicle registration numbers to customers at the time of delivery of the vehicles. It is not that others could not have done that but LML as a brand pioneered these and delighted the customers whereby all these attributes did not require deep research to get implemented.

3. **Each interaction is an opportunity to demonstrate Customer Delight**: The company has to make sure that the feeling of *satisfaction* as well as *satisfaction to delight* transition has to be experienced by the customers even when the product or service is not in picture. Moreover, once the product/service use has begun or it has reached post usage experience for the customer where, the customer is expected to use it regularly later on or to buy it afresh (one time use and throw/consume product), the company should ensure to put delight wherever it can. This requires a very professional frame of mind. This should be not only the feeling within the company employees but also with distributors, retailers as well as their employees. The company should ensure that whatever message of customer delight it is trying to

promote through its mass communication , it should get reflected in the first hand experience which the end user is having before buying the product/service, during buying it as well as after having bought it. Nestle as a company has tried to do it time and again. The beginnings of **Nescafé** can be traced all the way back to 1930, when the Brazilian government first approached Nestlé. Their coffee guru, Max Morgenthaler, and his team set out immediately to find a way of producing a quality cup of coffee that could be made simply by adding water, yet would retain the coffee's natural flavor. After seven long years of research in their Swiss laboratories, they found the answer. The new product was named **Nescafé** – a combination of Nestlé and café. They first introduced **Nescafé**, the first commercially successful soluble coffee, in Switzerland, on April 1st, 1938.For the first half of the next decade, however, World War II hindered its success in Europe. **Nescafé** was soon exported to France, Great Britain and the USA. Its popularity grew rapidly through the rest of the decade. By the 1950s, coffee had become the beverage of choice for teenagers, who were flocking to coffeehouses to hear the new rock 'n' roll music. Since those days and times till now, Nescafe as a brand from Nestle has carved a very strong impression on masses as far as quality hot coffee is concerned. It has tried to delight its customers at various touchpoints of its interaction. Advertising happens to be elegant as well as smooth with changing times.Moreover, all its communications look very fresh whether an offering is old or new.It clearly does justice to its basic message of freshness through all its offerings.

4. **Appreciate that being a good cause is no longer good enough**: Customer appreciates any organization which stands for a good cause over and above its business objective. But, it has to be translated into action regularly and the customer should be made to feel it directly as well as indirectly. Moreover, the company has to

make efforts to ensure that the customers believe its good cause and also believe that it is seriously committed towards it. The House of Tatas is reputed for good causes since long. Moreover, the company is also known for its ethical practices since its inception. It carries so well with its personality that with every product or service which company brings out from time to time, end-users as well as distribution people look at it with awe. The various causes for which Tatas have stood for and steadfastly adhered to are innumerable. With all these coming along with sound business decisions from time to time have always delighted the customers. Tata Motors continuously educates customers with these efforts which it does internally as well as externally with respect to the organization. This ensures it consistent respectful image in the minds of consumers. Tata Motors is involved with many exercises which come under *Green matters* and *Community development. Green matters* involve reduction of environmental pollution and regular pollution control drives. It also incorporates restoration of ecological balance It practices these things to the core by making and marketing its own vehicles as per the standards which it feels fit. Continuously working towards products which take care of these aspects and promoting affluent treatment facilities, nurturing greeneries in and around its plants, townships etc are all endeavors in this direction. *Community Development* service division of the company works through various societies to improve the conditions of neighboring villages encouraging economic independence through self-initiated cottage industries and contributing to community and social forestry, road construction, rural health, education, water supply and family planning.

5. Adequate is not acceptable: When we are talking and discussing about delight, the company has to ensure that it is not just providing solutions to consumers problems. In other words, the company should not just position itself or its products as adequate products. It should create some aspirational value behind its existence and should ensure that a section of consumers like it because it continuously brings new offerings and innovations for themselves and their lives. A very good example in this direction is the service offering from Qberoi Group of Hotels and Resorts. In exotic locations and faraway lands, Oberoi Hotels and Resorts are setting entirely new standards for the world of luxury hotel keeping. Combining traditional beauty with modern facilities, each Oberoi Hotel is the ultimate experience in every sense. Their commitment to excellence, attention to detail and personalized service has ensured a loyal guest list and worldwide acclaim .In their efforts to come very close to customers, the group has a very distinct bouquet of special offers which makes it go beyond what can be termed as adequate. It includes escape to fabulous resorts in locations where spectacular landscapes, historical wonders, magnificent beaches and wild adventure promise to create memories for a lifetime. Luxurious settings, impeccable service, international cuisine and pampering spa treatments come together to create the perfect holiday.

6. We must know who our customers are and what they want and how they want it:
The company should continuously take feedback from consumers so as to keep a check on their expectations and also take ideas from them in order to spring pleasant surprises in the form of new product developments, product modifications, service delivery etc. It is also important that the consumers are consciously reminded of their expectations from the company and at the same

time, they are unconsciouly moving their lives with the products and services of the company Nirulas have .established itself as a good name in discovering and re-discovering their customers continuously..Established in 1934, Nirula's today is a diversified group having a chain of Elegant Business Hotels, Waiter Service Restaurants, Family Style Restaurants, Ice Cream Parlours, Pastry Shops and Food Processing Plants in India. The chain caters to over 50,000 guests every day.

Delhi Times has honoured Nirula's, the oldest and largest Quick Service Restaurant chain in Delhi with the Times of India's "Dishy Man" Award. Long associated with quality food and service at reasonable prices, people at Nirula's pride themselves on providing Delhi with Value-for-Money products. Ever since its inception in 1934, Nirula's has grown with the times and catered to the changing food tastes of the Capital. Not only has it catered to Delhi's changing palate, Nirula's been instrumental in introducing the Dilli-wallah to the pizza, hot dog and other such items. The Chinese Room was the first Chinese food restaurant in the Capital to be run by non-Chinese people. Nirula's has expanded its repertoire from Indian foods to Western to Chinese to confectionery to ice creams. And all this at a time when such concepts were relatively unknown to Delhi's belly. Committed to serve Delhi's palate, Nirula's hopes to go on to achieve further heights in its endeavour.

7. Customer Delight is about story telling: There is no any big art or technical input required to make customer delight get conveyed to the customer. It can be made understandable to the customer in the most simple language and in the form of a story. Many times, a very sophisticated work done by a company is communicated in much more sophisticated language and it loads heavily on the ear of the end user or a probable end user. The company should ensure to communicate even the most path-breaking activity in the simplest language possible. Lipton has done this with the most finesse. Its advertisements communicate its utility and health value in the most simple manner. Its latest TV Commercial says "The tea leaf....could it make the best beverage in the world? Naturally refreshing. Naturally protective.LIPTON.® Tea Can Do That".It is supported with the visual of a smart man and woman consuming tea and feeling relaxed. Not many words used and not much head breaking required by the viewer to understand a very strong message conveyed in a simple manner.

8. Customer Delight starts at the top: It is very much pertinent for everyone in the company to realize that customer delight will work if a top down approach is seriously implemented. In other words, it cannot be left on the middle or junior level employees to make customer delight happen with the top brass showing no interest in it. They have to not only show interest in the endeavor, but become the most prolific spokesperson as well as the guide for the exercise in the future. Ensuring customer delight at times require certain policy decision changes, massive investments etc which may not fructify without the ownership and involvement of the top management. General Electric has perfected this art to the core. Its days of Jack Welch as CEO are much talked about. In fact, it continues vigorously on the path of owning efforts related to ensuring customer delight in whichever product or service category it is present. GE strives to create a balance between the value that employees contribute to the Company and the rewards offered in return. GE fulfills this goal by fostering a work environment where good ideas and a strong work ethic are encouraged throughout the Company. At the heart of this dynamic culture is an investment in learning. GE employees are both expected and encouraged to fulfill training that helps them navigate a more competitive marketplace, learn domain expertise, develop skills and comply with the Company's integrity and citizenship initiatives. GE reflects the many communities in which it operates. GE fosters a diverse workforce and is making strides in increasing the representation of women and minorities as a percentage of the workforce and in management. As a global company, GE is also sensitive to the importance of protecting the privacy of employees and to enabling flexible work arrangements that accommodate the way that people work today. While they have made continuous improvements in all of these arenas, their size and the breadth of their businesses besides the dynamic pace in which they operate means a lot. They are completely aware to remain committed to facilitating an ongoing dialogue with employees to refine their approach in order to nurture their success as well as organizational success..

9. For Customer Delight to work, an environment of empowerment must exist: When we have talked about ownership and involvement of top management in the exercise related to customer delight, it also means that other levels of management as well as the distribution network responsible in the field should be having certain well defined powers so that customer delight passes smoothly at all levels and everyone involved in its implementation owns up all developments in this direction. Hindustan Levers Limited is known to foster this culture in its operations. Corporate Social Responsibility (CSR) in Hindustan Lever Limited (HLL) is rooted in its Corporate Purpose - the belief that "to succeed requires the highest standards of corporate behaviour towards our employees, consumers and the societies and world in which we live". HLL's CSR philosophy is embedded in its commitment to all stakeholders - consumers, employees, the environment and the society that the organisation operates in. HLL believes that it is this commitment which will deliver sustainable, profitable growth. Unilever is committed to diversity in a working environment where there is mutual trust and respect and where everyone feels responsible for the performance and reputation of the company.The company recruits, employ and promote employees on the sole basis of the qualifications and abilities needed for the work to be performed. It is committed to safe and healthy working conditions for all employees. The Company does not use any form of forced, compulsory or child labour. They are committed to working with employees to develop and enhance each individual's skills and capabilities.They respect the dignity of the individual and the right of employees to freedom of association. They maintain good communications with employees through company based information and consultation procedures. Unilever is committed to establishing mutually beneficial relations with its suppliers, customers and business partners. In their business dealings ,partners are expected to adhere to business principles consistent with their own

10. It is all about behavior and not about structure or position: The Customer at any stage of involvement respects an organization for its approach towards coming closer to him/her and not on the basis of what is the structural arrangement of the company. Consumer expects behavior of all the stages of involvement right from the company and passing through distributer/dealer on to retailer to be exemplary and beyond average. In fact, if this is ensured, even if the product or service per se is not having any delight to offer, this behavior will itself delight the consumer. McDonalds works hard in making such a behavior exist round the clock at its various locations. Relevant, user-friendly, motivational information is a key part of their balanced, active lifestyles approach. building on its more than 30-year history of providing nutrition information

McDonalds is expanding its efforts to help customers make food and fitness choices that are right for them. They are providing more types of information through a variety of communications vehicles. The Company understand that, to educate children, they must communicate with them in a fun and meaningful way. Ronald McDonald once taught children to fasten their safety belts. Now his set up teaches them to eat well and live active lives. Many of McDonald's local business units also offer in-restaurant nutrition information in brochures. They are making nutrition information accessible and relevant in other ways. For example:

- Trayliners have been used to provide nutrition information and balanced, active lifestyles tips in a number of local markets, including **Hong Kong**, the **Netherlands**, and **France**.

- McDonald's **Canada** provides nutrition information for menu items on posters at the front counter.

- McDonald's **Germany** distributes quarterly flyers with questions and answers on food quality, nutrition, and energy balance.

McDonalds **U.S.** business offers wallet cards that show nutritional values and food exchanges. As part of their global balanced, active lifestyles education campaign, they plan to add wellness tips to Happy Meal and standard packaging in major markets around the world

11. Staff and volunteers are partners and not customers: The company has to consider its own staff members as partners and not as customers. Same goes with volunteers who promote the company products. It means that every stage of delight and its communication to all audiences should be done with active involvement of staff people. At no point of time it should happen that staff members are left clueless about delight and related happenings. Knowledge sharing with staff members should be regular so that during their dealings with the members of distribution channels, they are able to handle all queries, discussions and any product related happenings with ease and confidence. ICICI Bank is doing this exercise with very organized rigor. The bank ensures that staff and volunteers are taken into complete confidence and knowledge sharing with them gets done in the most professional manner so that customers are handled with ease at any touch-point of the institution.

12. Customer Delight is a process not an event: It should be made clear to everyone involved with the company, inside as well as outside the company that delight is not a happening but a continuous process. It means that the customer as well as end-user should feel that delight before using the product/service and this should continue while using it and it should remain with him/her after he/she has used it (consumed it in case of one time product) or kept it for re-use again in case of consumer durable). In other words, customer or end user should take a product/ service usage as part of his/her daily routine in order to make her /him feel the delight. Walddisney vacations does just that with its potential customers. It seeps into the customers psyche and makes his or her experience so pleasant that it is remembered for long times to come. It invites the potential customer for a vacation in Orlando and visit the many theme parks, including Disney World, that makes Orlando the tourist destination of the world. It further says in its communication that some of its vacation packages include theme park tickets to Disney World, Universal Studios, Sea World and others. Further on it gives links to related websites for online reservations or details of useful postal addresses for physical reservations. All this happens much before the experience has not even begun.

References

"The Instinctive Corporaton-Delight as the Basis of Customer Satisfaction", Vinay

Kamat, *The Times of India ,August 13,1999 & Sept 23,2004*

http://www.associationworks.com/customerdelight.htm

www.marutiswift.com

www.lmlindia.com

www.nestle.com

www.tatamotors.com

www.oberoihotels.com

www.nirula.com

www.lipton.com

www.ge.com

www.hll.com

www.mcdonalds.com

www.icicibank.com

www.walddisney.com

12. **Marketing Strategically to Rural Indian folks: A basket full of opportunities**

(This Paper was presented at 9th Convention of Strategic Management Forum on **"Strategic Management: Current Research Efforts and Future Challenges** during May 18-20, 2006 held at Indian Institute of Management, Kozhikode, Kerala,India)

Statements, views, opinions and comments about marketing keep pouring in from time to time. Each one is debatable by virtue of being subjective in nature. Marketing professionals themselves do not agree most of the times on these aspects. Precisely ,because of this ,there is always a room for controversy surrounding marketing as a discipline. Its controversial nature makes it challenging as well as fascinating to all those concerned as well as unconcerned. Further when one considers the potential of marketing to rural India, the imaginations can be mind-boggling. Whether we go deep into the Environment of Marketing ,Consumer Buying Behavior or Industrial Buying Behavior, New Product Development, Advertising and Promotion Management, Sales and Distribution Management, Pricing, Branding, Market Research etc., the challenge is everywhere. With the rural hinterland having its own set of complexities which keep on changing as we travel from any part of our country to any other part, this complexity not only is a challenge but also a huge opportunity for marketers of all hues. With effect from April 1,2001, as Quantitative restrictions on all items of import in all categories gone, the entire industry in all product categories has to accept the challenge and face it head-on. No longer is the safe umbrella of state protection available for our manufacturers and marketers. The mantra is either to face the challenge and perform or exit. I'll throw some light on certain areas in Marketing Management to support the , fascination & challenge it offers with respect to marketing to rural folks

Nature of Market: The market is characterized by large volumes but low margins. High incomes combined with low cost of living in the villages have meant more money to spend. Rural folks are also expecting value for money continuously. They are willing to go for premium brands in any product category. Tastes are also changing. To illustrate in a simple manner, detergent cakes and single-edged blades have given way to detergent powders and twin blades. One can easily find Whisper sanitary napkins, Kellogg's com flakes and other premium products on rural stores. It can be definitely attributed to a slow but sure erosion of price sensitivity. But the companies have to give importance to the fact that there is a complete absence of middle class in the rural market. *There are mainly the rich and the poor in the villages.*

Rural Market Segments:

Rural market can be broadly segmented into three

categories: .

. Premium niche segment

. Premium and value-for-money segment .

Value-for-money segment

Consumer Behavior and Marketing Research:

No matter whatever may be the trend, consumer buying behavior will forever remain a fascinating and challenging aspect for marketers. *The popular image of a rural consumer is of one who has limited educational background, is exposed to limited products and brands ,choosing price over quality and is influenced by word-of- mouth communication.* The influences on the behavior of the rural consumer is also changing. The lifestyle of rural consumers is influenced by:

a. Increasing incomes and income distribution

b. Marketers efforts to reach out and educate potential consumers.

c. The situation in which he or she utilizes the product.

Moreover, the place of purchase and variations in it play a significant role at different times.

Rural consumers do not rely on the local outlets and *haats(rural markets)* alone as some of the

purchases are made in urban areas.

Understanding the social and attitudinal influences on rural consumer is important to the

marketer, as these serve as a guide to decisions on product offering, pricing, distribution, and

media and message which ultimately forms the 'rural marketing strategy

With consumer behavior, one cannot ignore the relevance of researching the rural consumer

thoroughly. The tools and techniques for researching rural markets remain the same but these

need modifications in application in line with the differences from the urban markets. A

researcher of rural markets will find it useful to have a research design that compares urban and

rural markets besides reflecting rural consumer behavior. Participatory Rural Appraisal(PRA) is

a suitable method. In this method, dimensions and measures are identified by the researcher

instead of being imposed by the researcher. In- depth interviews are preferred over structured

interviews or questionnaires as the former increase the validity of the data obtained by allowing

the respondent flexibility to express an opinion within the frame of reference. Decisions related

to specific aspects like responses to brand names, packaging, specific attributes and pricing can

be arrived at by using experimental methods of research In the sampling method, one approach

is to select a representative village. Then, a sample from that village population reflecting the

over-all profile of the village population is subjected to survey tools related to the requirement of

the study-general or specific. Once that is done, data collected is subjected to analytical tools and findings arrived at. It looks same as a research done in urban settings, but it is different due to some different variables involved.

Competition: Companies in general and Marketers in particular may not like to face this word but they know that the reality is exactly opposite. It is this competition which has made them marketers who are always on the move. There is a lot of hue and cry about local goods flooding the markets at various levels and giving big companies a run for their money. There is a mystery surrounding their cheap products in all categories. All the big companies in India have to accept certain hard facts in this direction. Firstly, the competition is with companies of the same level and not with locally made or cheaply produced stuff.. Secondly, the basics for every big company to promote and sustain products in rural markets remain the same. If HLL is present in some rural markets, then P&G has to find ways and means to counter HLL than to waste its energies on fighting some local player who does not fall anywhere near its quality or reach ability.

Sales promotion:

In rural markets people don't have a let-go approach and a very sophisticated tool with respect to urban markets may fall flat on the face of the company in a rural arena. While applying sales promotion in rural markets, companies can link them with religious festivities which are an almost regular feature throughout the year in any rural surrounding.

Services Marketing*:

With more and more services coming into limelight and innovating from time to

time, it is very important for players in this segment to find ways and means to come more

closer to consumers before the competitor/s do it. Whether it is the hospitality industry,

educational services or consultancies where service is the product or the after sales service

wings of companies producing tangible products, it applies everywhere. The challenge lies in

ensuring no complaints but more challenging is the scenario in which you face complaints vis-a-

vis your products which are handled and this handling itself becomes a marketing strategy

for the future. This activity is done every time a complaint comes. The complaint may be

related to the product, or to the delivery date or even to its packaging etc. It happens many times

that a complaint is taken as a deadly development by. marketers which will damage the

company for a long time. On the other hand, a deft and prompt handling of the complaint

will not only redeem the faith of the consumer in the company but will also generate a favorable word

of mouth by him/her for other existing as well as potential consumers.

Retailing:

This is the area which is passing through a lot of churning in the present times. With more and

more firms coming in retailing, it requires more and more marketers with skills in counter

selling besides field selling. At times, retail selling is also looked down upon by convention

al marketing and sales people. Moreover the parties which are coming into retailing with huge

investments are expecting fast returns and training of employees is either totally ignored or done

in a haphazard manner. According to A.T.Kearney (global management consultants), retail

business in India for the year 2000 was Rs 400000 crore and it was estimated to reach Rs

800000 crore by the year 2005. This retail boom can be attributed to a burgeoning middle class

in India. According to Ronald J. Floto, group chief executive, Dairy Farm Group, "The growth

of the middle class is critical to the growth of retailing." This has happened in India. According to McKinsey, over the last decade, India's middle and high income populatjon (defined as households with an annual income of over Rs 60,000) has grown at a rapid pace of over 10 percent per annum, even as the large low-income base has shrunk. Here lies the challenge of making these neo-middle and upper class section walk in retail stores and clinch the deal/s.
 A very significant aspect here is customer retention over a longer period of time.
Earlier when retail was not an important tool of marketing for many players, all those into it were having good traffic which got converted into buyers many times. But with number of retail outlets multiplying, the competition is increasing and fascination for retailing has become a challenge. All the players have to develop that brand loyalty in the same way as has been done for ages for tangible products. The growth of the retail industry clearly indicates that in the next ten years, nearly one million new jobs will be created in the organized retail sector(ICFAI Research center). So, going by the investments and predictions, the challenge is there but it requires a proper mindset to handle this challenge with care. It applies to all involved whether promoters or employees or government etc.

Communicating with the Rural Markets:

This aspect has posed enormous challenges to the rural marketer. The problem primarily is related to a large number of consumers scattered across the country. Moreover, many of these are not attuned to the mass media. Variations in these markets occur by geography, demography, selective perception or retention of individuals, the level of involvement in purchase behavior and state of readiness. Companies from time to time have used varied strategies which serve as a ready reckoner for others to follow. Nirma uses the television route for advertising its detergents which are beamed to rural audiences and ONIDA's commercial on the magic of black and white television portrays its message. Moreover, the information seeking and processing behavior of the rural consumer influence the media and the message. A number of factors affect the effectiveness of a message. The message for the rural market has to reflect the framework that is meaningful to the rural consumer. It thereby makes it necessary to give importance to language, pictorial presentation and the lucid form of the message with respect to the rural audience giving due importance to the credibility of the message source as well association of products with certain rural contexts. Dabur found it very effective to distribute religious texts like ~Hanurnan Chalisa and Rarncharitmanas or calendars with religious themes along with its ayurvedic products(Das Gupta and Menon,1990).A soil conditioner called Terracare uses popular figures from mythology images to attract the rural consumer(Ghosh and fKrishnaswarny, 1997).

Product and Price as Strategic variables: ~A marketing strategy for rural markets focuses on products tailored to the needs of these consumers. The other way round could be to offer an existing product in urban areas at a lower price to price sensitive consumers. It all depends upon the organizations' ability to meet the consumer needs effectively. Product strategy decisions include product-market selection and positioning. Decisions on the product range and its features are required to support the selected product-market and the positioning. The ability to utilize the opportunities in rural markets depend upon others, on cost-effectiveness and the reach of distribution of products in the rural markets. Nirma was the first to tap the opportunity in the rural market for detergent powder through its catchy promotion. However, when Wheel, another detergent powder, was introduced in the same market, it created a dent in Nirma' s market indicating the potency of an effective strategy based on channel resources. Besides this, it is also to be accepted that rural markets are not homogeneous. There is a need for creating and offering product variants to meet the different needs within the rural markets.In rural ambiences, demonstrating the product is an effective way to educate and position the product in the consumer's mind. *This method is used extensively to meet the challenge of generic competition and brand competition.* The Colgate advertisement of the wrestler with the weak tooth is targeted at users of charcoal powder and local tooth powder. It not only encourages rural folks to switch over to its brand but also directly competes with unbranded players spread in rural area at various levels. Education on the benefits of various products is

also very common in rural markets. It has been widely practiced with shampoos. Shampoos are positioned as convenient, replacing the traditional soapnut or even soap in the rural market. Hindustan Lever's campaign to wash shirts or shampoo the villagers hair free are instances of product education. : Perception of consumers in rural markets may vary..The size, shape, color, enduring smell and taste generate different set of response for the urban and the rural consumers. Most pressure cookers are designed with handles on one side, which is fine if there is a controllable flame and the person cooking remains standing while preparing a meal, typical in an urban kitchen. But, this pressure cooker is very unwieldy in a rural kitchen where a typical rural household uses an open fire or *chulha* with the person cooking squatting on the ground. *The rural housewife may dream of some day owning a gas stove, (but meanwhile she needs a wide-bodied cooker with handles on opposite sides. Marketers, are you hearing?* In the same vein, radios, cassette players and television sets
are made to urban power supply specifications. In many villages, particularly in power- strapped states, voltages fluctuate wildly making these products susceptible to frequent breakdowns. If products like the television or radio can withstand wide voltage fluctuations, consumers would not mind paying more for reliability. Efforts to develop products that suit the rural environment are Cadbury's chocolates that do not melt so easily in the heat and LML's scooter with a more powerful engine aimed at the farmer which he can use for transporting goods(Das Gupta and Menon, 1990) On the pricing
front, it is also not always true that only cheap brands sell in rural markets. Usha found that the sale of its economy models were falling sharply in rural areas. Farmers prefer Usha's premier Century brand, though it is priced 20 percent higher(Das Gupta and Menon, 1990).
Branded goods comprise 65 percent of sales in villages and the share of non-branded products is shrinking dramatically. In the case of convenience goods, sachets or low unit packs have generated a new sales wave for branded products. The rural brands are mostly recognized through symbols, logos and colour be it the 'Billi walli cell'(battery with a cat as a symbol-

Eveready), 'Lal saboon'(red soap-Lifebuoy Soap). Building a brand personality so as to stand out in a product category can be very tough, however the process of rural branding involves basically three steps. One, creating an identity, second, enhancing recognition and third, building a brand image. All the players in rural market follow these albeit with some differentiation here and there.

E-Marketing: It is having many names in the form of B2B, B2C etc. But what matters is the effectiveness of the marketing efforts on the internet which has made it fascinating as well as challenging. This has become more intensified as there is almost no any human interaction involved while the exercise is on. No matter whatever may be the brand personality offline, to make it online, an information- rich site that consumers find genuinely useful is the only way. The online experience must support the offline experience. If we as marketers allow consumers to e-mail to us via a web site, we must respond to them. If information takes too long to download or crashes their computer, or if our site is badly designed, then it will make the consumers carry similar impressions about the offline brand. The first question any company contemplating a presence on the web must answer is why it wants to be there. Is it to sell products (e-commerce), or build the brand (I-branding), or to save money (e-operation) ? The acid test for a truly successful site depends on how involved the customer becomes with the brand on-line. On an average how long does he stay on the site, and what reasons, if any , are there for him to come back. ? The emphasis should lie on how to use the potential of the Net to develop an on-going two way dialogue with the consumer, rather than posting standard information on the site that resembles a brochure. In B2B marketing, the issue of pricing has been the biggest bugbear. Now its realized that the customer is not always seeking the lowest price. In the words of Partha Iyengar, country manager, Gartner Group, "The B2B portals have incorrectly assumed-like the rest of the world-that a steady market for customers exIst."

Marketers here have to create desire and utility in the mindsets of the chief decision-makers in old as well as new economy to use internet for buying and selling either through independent portals or through establishing their own e- marketing division. In other words, either match the brands online and offline or . don't have it online. If the brand exists only online, then such problems should be tackled more fast. With respect to rural markets, this gains lot of credibility thru making masses use computers, ensuring Internet availability with the input of local language for communication

Ethics in Marketing:

As there is a darker side to every issue, same can be said about marketing. At the same time, it is not the discipline of Marketing per se which is bad, but some practitioners and promoters at times commit blunders thereby bringing the whole subject area into disrepute. It has to be corrected and I'm all for it. I'll now be highlighting certain examples where marketing acquired a bad name and the question of ethics came into picture. Who can forget the Tuffs shoe advertisement by Phoenix in mid-90s in which Milind Soman and Madhu Sapre were shown entwined with almost nothing to cover their bodies except a snake swirling all over them besides sporting a pair of the shoe advertised. It created a hue and cry and ultimately the objectionable parts of the print ad were covered in the future releases in magazines etc. This ad tried to promote a product by using sex appeal and that too in an obscene manner. We also find companies fighting over ethical issues and later on agree to bury the issue as well as ethics itself thereby caring a damn for the consumer. The classic example in this direction is that of a case between HLL and Fena on the detergent bar which showed how both the companies levelled charges on one another's promotions on television, making a big issue of ethical concern for the end-user' and even taking one another to court thereby making consumers feel important. But just when consumers started feeling important ,both the companies agreed to settle the matter 'amicably' and bury the hatchet ,thereby letting ethics go to dogs. Another very significant issue here is the public concern. 1997 was a watershed year for the roads and road users of Delhi. Supreme Court got convinced of the strong relationship between the number of accidents on Delhi roads & the hoardings of all sizes with ads of different companies almost choking the skyline of our National Capital. These hoardings were banned and long continuous stretch of the Ring Road started giving a good drive and uninterrupted flow of traffic to Delhi-ites with their mind and eyes becoming free of any distraction. The number of accidents also got reduced dramatically. In early 2000s in Ahmedabad, Navratri celebrations saw Pan masala companies keeping a distance from the ceremonies as per the directive from authorities which felt that a product having tobacco content should not be seen as a part of celebrations. A debate is also going on the way in which makers of Dandi salt have used a pictorial depiction of the famous Dandi Yatra led by Mahatma Gandhi on the packet itself. It is seen ethical as well unethical by people who are divided according to their interpretations. By quoting these examples, I mean to say that the activity of marketing and the work of marketers is welcome but it should be accompanied with a responsibility and concern for the society. Otherwise, there are a lot of sticks with which we as marketers can be made responsible e.g., consumer forum, courts etc.

Strategies for Rural Marketing:

Whether it is rural or urban market, a strategy remains more or less the same. What differs is the application of it in different surroundings. In simple words, surroundings can be termed as environment. A market environment consists of factors and forces that effect an organization's ability to develop and maintain successful transactions and relationships with target customers. The micro part of this environment is made up of suppliers, buyers, competitors, facilitators and other influence groups. On the other hand, the macro part includes domestic and international business environment, social, cultural and demographic aspects of the market, technological and natural environment besides the political and legal aspects. Now, farmer economics should be the guiding force in implementing the rural marketing strategy. It involves product, place, price as well as promotion and a judicious mix of all of these.

Conclusion:

At the end, I will like to mention that there are so many areas in Marketing which make it an interesting and important discipline in all types of industrial activities. My observations may not have covered all the finer aspects of marketing, but I've frankly put forward my views in certain areas as above. Rural marketing is definitely going to be challenging for whichever company already ventured in to it as well to all others planning to plunge into it.

References:

I. Rajshekhar M, *The elusive money with the rural super rich,* Businessworld, July 28, 2003 Pgs 64-66

2 Velayudhan, S.N. (2002). Rural Marketing: Targeting the Non Urban Consumer. New Delhi: Response Books.

3 Rajagopal (2003), Rural Marketing: Development,Policy,Planning & Practice. Jaipur. Rawat Publications

4 Sukhpal Singh(2001), Rural Marketing Management,New Delhi, Vikas Publishing House Pvt Ltd

5 C S G Krishnamacharyulu, Lalitha Rarnakrishnan(2003), Cases in Rural Marketing: An Integrated Approach, New Delhi: Pearson Education

6. Ramkishen Y(2002), New Perspectives on Rural Marketing;includes agricultural marketing, Mumbai. Jaico Publishing House

13. Branding Star Hotels -A Conceptual Framework with reference to Ahmedabad

(This Paper was presented at   Fourth AIMS International Conference On Management on the Theme "Managing Global Organizations: Challenges, Opportunities and Strategies" during December 28-31, 2006, held at Indian Institute of Management Indore, M.P,India)

It is therefore significant to work on all the tangibles so that hotel branding gets moving successfully. Branding exercise in Star hotels have to consider factors which exist outside the hotel as well as inside the hotel. The package of these factors work interdependently and not in isolation. Promoters of hotels have to continuously ensure the interdependency of factors in and out of the hotel so that branding becomes strong ,everlasting and continuous . This paper takes a journey   into these factors in order to come up with a branding mix for star hotels. Off-course the framework will depend upon the various general and specific factors to function or not. We will go into the detail of various factors which can and must contribute in the direction of branding star hotels.

1. **Architecture;** This is the most significant aspect of branding any star hotel. Some of the hotels tout this feature and the detailing which this feature has gone through which has attracted customers from all over the world. Actually speaking, architecture involves the layout from   inside as well as the outside of the hotel. In fact, it lends the ambience to all the nooks and corners of the entire hotel .It is given a serious thought at the beginning because it cannot be altered once it has been put into reality. Only cosmetic changes can be applied but the main architecture cannot be altered. The hotel   takes pride in its exquisite architecture and makes it felt by its guests through various ways. It also happens that guests having stayed in a hotel take its architecture through their memories, photos, video films etc with them to far off places from where they come and spread a very positive word of mouth. It is not necessary that for a very good architecture , huge space is required for a star hotel. There are numerous examples where a multi-storied star hotel is located in a very small ground space but its architecture is known across the world. Architecture also relates to the uniqueness of the country and the region where the property is located. It does a world of good to the property if its promoters highlight the architectural uniqueness of the country

or the region etc in the exterior as well as the interior of the hotel. This way, a service is done not only to the architectural splendor of the country but also to the guest who identifies it without going into the origin of that architecture itself.

2. **Stunning lobby:** The lobby happens to be the first interface of any good star hotel. It helps in guest Imagery of what is in store for him or her. Lobby is symbolized with a deafening degree of quietness. It happens to be the place where most of the dealing between the guest/s and the hotel take place and it has to remain in quiet mode. It is ironical but it happens coolly and comfortably. Mondrian Hotel, Los Angeles captures this beautifully. By uniting a love of nature, the outdoors, and casual living with a profound sense of glamour and fantasy, Mondrian captures the quintessential California lifestyle Mondrian's lobby is an inspired and surreal stage set with diaphanous curtains, Glowing glass walls, eclectic furnishings, and a stunning Indoor/Outdoor Lobby that seems to magically transport the indoors out and the outdoors in. One very significant aspect of a good lobby is the controlled quietness which has to be ensured. The place serves the purpose of a break from the room and outdoor where the guests as well as their business and leisure visitors relax and re -coup. At times, lobby also serves as a waiting lounge for visitors and guests who have to check in. Hotel authorities have to ensure that this waiting period should not disrupt the tranquility and calm of the lobby at any cost. If it requires some curt instructions at times, so be it. Lobby also requires some decorative ambience with light music going on. Decorative ambience should be simple in the form of good wall-size paintings, murals, artistic center tables with vases etc. All hotels ensure such type of things but what matters is its effective layout and positioning different things in the space available. If the space permits and the construction is fine, a waterway can be a part of the lobby. However, a waterway may not be there in all hotel lobbies.

3. **Sheer elegance:** This aspect of any star hotel covers everything from its public   relations exercise till the guest has experienced his/her stay and carries his/her experiences as word of mouth and comes again as well as encourages others to come. Elegance relates to a definite style which gets embodied in a hotel and all its

patrons. It implies a dignified persona where each and every resource (human or otherwise) reflects etiquette, mannerisms and sophistication even when simplicity and humbleness are also there.

4. **Color scheme:** Colors add so many things in an individuals personality. In the same vein colors can add many facets into the overall perception, personality as well as experiences with a star hotel. Here, it is important to mention   that colors are not only in the external look of the hotel but also in each and every internal construction, design as well as layout.

5. **Wall-sized murals in each room:** It requires a story to be told when one enters and stays in the room of a star hotel. Big walls cannot be left blank staring at the guest. Murals add a story and an aesthetic touch to the guest whether for any business purpose or for leisure or even for a combination of both. But it is very important for the hotel set up to decide which type of mural to be put in which type   of accommodation. It goes for a stylish restaurant also. Manhattans newest historic   restaurant, Murals on 54 features innovative continental cuisine with international   influences. The modernized dining room is warm and comfortable and showcases Dean Cornwell's historic murals painted in 1937. The murals were just meticulously restored in February 2004.

6. **Custom designed furniture:** The more aesthetic the mood in the hotel , the more design goes into the furniture. Even the vice-versa is also true many times if not always.

7. **Musical score:** Music adds to the elegance of any location. When the location is a star hotel, it becomes more elegant when the whole of hotel interior is having a soothing music going on round the clock.

8. **Retail design concepts such as quarterly change-outs of reception art and signage to keep things fresh:** Change is the only constant in this world. Even a star hotel should change internally by redesigning reception or signage etc with the objective of communicating dynamism.

9. **In-room High-speed Internet Access:** Internet and its use has become a necessity with any class of traveler in modern times. Hotel should ensure high speed internet connectivity with privacy inside every room.

10. **Events and Experiences**: With a brand name attached to it and a strong presence in the city and in some cases across the country and the whole world, the hotel branding gets enhanced through conducting ,endorsing, hosting or co-hosting events and experiences.

11. **Sales Promotion**; A marketing tool which applies for short durations can be effectively used by a star hotel for different periods of time depending upon the period and its importance. It is very important to make the sales promotion tool connect well with the brand personality of the hotel and the expectation of its clientele.

12. **Mass Communication**: Referring basically to advertising, the star ranking should make this communication tool more and more classy through packing information, data, desire, passion, class and heritage besides the experience of serving customers for long in its communication mix.

With these factors in mind, we tried to find from Hotel fraternity in Ahmedabad as to what they do and what they have to say about all this.

Le Meridian

The performance of Le Meridian on various parameters of Star hotel branding

Le Meridien hotels are mostly *atrium* type of hotels, with special emphasis being on the lobby of the hotel. As per the hotel authorities , lobby is the most important part of the hotel, because it is primary area where customer comes in close contact with the property, and makes the first impression about the property. This aspect is very well taken care of at Ahmedabad property also.

The *color combination* of the hotel is a blend of Dark and light colors. The property at Ahmedabad being more oriented towards business travelers, the colors are mostly urban in nature with dark furniture (sofas being Dark black in color) to maintain the perfect match, balancing the forces of Ying and Yang.

Elegance forms an important aspect of Le Meridien, which becomes obvious with the kind of décor maintained inside the lobby, and the same is taken care off for the room also, the staff is well groomed and attentive to the needs of visitors, travelers and guests alike. Even the glasses in which water is served are covered with quality coverings.

Murals do form an important part of the Le Meridien not only in the lobby but also in gangways or what are also known as approach to the rooms. In the rooms, murals do exist but are smaller in size. Flower vases are a common site in rooms.

Custom designed furniture is virtually non existent as far as Ahmedabad property is concerned.

Musical score is of course part of branding exercise, the difference being that more energetic music is played in the morning and a lighter tone during evenings and nights. The concept being that as mornings are a little hectic, it is important that guests as well as employees get motivated to work better and faster with evenings being more relaxed after a tiring day.

Le meridian is *Wi-Fi enabled* and has internet accessibility also.

Design concepts do change but are not changed frequently and the average time period is 2-3 years for particular designs .Special decorations are done during festival seasons where special emphasis is given to the relevant theme of the festival.

External branding is done mainly through in house contacts and personal contacts of the manager and   the clientele is mostly corporate in Ahmedabad.

Mass communication is only done during special events for promoting the event.

Brand building is done by taking extra care of customers by knowing their likes and dislikes through keeping their previous records in the form of Management Information system (MIS).

Taj Ummed Residency

a. About Taj Group of Hotels:

- Taj group (sister companies of Tata Sons)
- Over 100 years old group, started with Taj Mahal, Mumbai in 1904
- 4 different kind of hotels targeting different segments

  - Taj hotels, resorts & palaces
  - Taj business hotels
  - Gateway hotels
  - Ginger

Taj hotels, resorts & palaces are for the specialized niche market targeting people from higher and upper class.

Taj business hotels are, for upper class business people, second in the ladder after Taj hotels, resorts & palaces.

Gateway hotels are below Taj business hotels in term of infrastructure
and services and they do not carry Taj name or logo.

Ginger is new concept by Taj. It's no-frills, low budget, self service kind of
hotels with trendy look. (night stay below 1000 Rs. anywhere in India)
Taj is estimating around 70 ginger hotels till the end of 2008.

b About Taj Ummed Residency, Ahmedabad:

- *Pricing*: Highest pricing matrix among all hotels in the city

- *Perceived as the best hotel* by the class of its target audience

- *Competitors:* Le Meridian, Pride Hotel and Fortune Landmark Hotel

- *Market share calculation*: average occupancy x average room rate

  Some figures quoted for the month of September 2006 with comparative figures of competitors are shown as below:

Hotel	Occupancy	Average Rate per room (Rs.)	Market Share(Rs)
Taj	91	4950	450450
Le Meridian	61	3350	204350
Pride	110	3100	341000
Fortune Landmark	N.A.	3600	---------

Even if we ignore Fortune Landmark, we can see the figure of Taj at the
Highest

- *Interior*: Different interiors and architecture in different hotels (according to space available as most of the
  hotels have been developed in existing buildings or palaces and not constructed from scratch)

- *Color scheme*: All group hotels use Earth colours (Red, brown, rust etc.) and thus this kind of color scheme is part of Taj identity

- **Branding efforts**:

Association with all international travel magazines

Advertisements only for some food festivals or such events

Participation in media interviews in big way

Remain in news for one or another reason

Advertising expenditure : Rs 350 cr / annum with The Times of India

A. *Re-launch of Indian Specialty Restaurant (Narmada)*

It was done in two stages

1. *In the first stage*, Taj invited the top restaurant and hotel spenders and other very top executives with their families e.g.: Mr. Piruz Khambhata of Rasna They were asked to come and taste different food items and their inputs were invited for finalizing the menu for new Narmada

2. *In the second stage*, the same people were invited at the launch of new Narmada. They were shown as to how their inputs were considered and how new Narmada has become their kind of restaurant.These families were gifted recipe booklets, special food masalas etc.

B. *Gift on the new venture of Shell*

Taj came to know that Shell group was going to use their own tankers instead of using tankers on rent

Taj guys visited Shell and took photographs of these newly bought tankers

Then, special cakes were prepared in the same tanker shape with logo of Shell and were gifted to all Shell offices all over India.

HOTEL PRIDE

The Brand 'PRIDE' and its USP:

- the biggest room inventory (110 rooms)

- the largest banquet (6 halls, one of them with capacity for 1000 people)

- 24 hr check in – check out facility

- the 'total corporate' hotel

Other Features:

- located in the most happening area (surrounded by multiplexes and malls) of Ahmedabad city

- 24 hr coffee shop and occasional mid-night buffet facility

- multi-cuisine restaurant – 'Bhandhini' (right now it was having 'Sham-e Avadh' concept and it was having all décor and ambience accordingly. Pride comes out with such different concepts at different point of time which adds to the experience of customers)

- specialized in non-veg. food

- completely wi-fi enabled

Branding Efforts:

- heavy advertising and promotions have been done in last two years to create the brand 'Pride'

- except Audio-visual media, all sort of media are used to promote the brand

- hefty discounts are given to permanent clients (corporates) on room-nights basis

- total 600 companies are associated with pride (due to rigorous branding and marketing efforts)

- participation (as official or non-official sponsors) in big events   e.g. Pride was official sponsor of 'Travel Tourism' Fair last year

- organizes events and food festivals regularly   e.g. Dhoom – 2006 (organized On 31st December, 2005, having DJ-dancing and mocktails) .It was big success

- planning for same kind of event (Dhoom – 2007) this time

Conclusion:

The various parameters which are used to brand any star hotel vary from property to property and there cannot be a standard model behind that. It is a combination of parameters intrinsic as well as extrinsic to a hotel . However, in Ahmedabad, the three premier hotels which were studied harped more on the external aspects related to customer/guest interface in general as well as event based partnership and sponsorships in order to build brand persona and ride over it.

Acknowledgement:

1 Special thanks to following students of mine for conducting interviews with Senior

Executives of some hotels in Ahmedabad

a. Deval Patel   MBA-2005-2007 Sem IV

b. Prakash Sharma MBA-2005-2007 Sem IV

2 Special Thanks to following Senior Executives who readily gave there valuable time to be interviewed by my students

a. Mr Sharad   Hotel Taj Ummed Resdency, Ahmedabad

c. Mr Makrand   Hotel Le Meridian, Ahmedabad

d. Mr Pritam   Hotel Pride, Ahmedabad

References:

http://www.hospitalitynet.org/news/4021425.search?query=hospitality+branding

http://www.hotelindigo.com/

http://www.tourismreview.com.au/

http://www.starwoodhotels.com/dp/en_US/corporate/comp_over.jsp

http://www.shanerhotels.com/homepage/index.phtml

http://www.hotel-online.com/Trends/Andersen/1998_BrandingF&B.html#outsourcing

http://www.hotelinteractive.com/hi_index.asp?page_id=5000&article_id=1157

www.barcelona-tourist-guide.com

www.mondrianhotel.com

http://www.traditional-building.com/brochure/members/colordesign.shtml

http://www.murals54.com/

http://www.warwickhotelny.com/s17145/murals.html

14. Branding of B-Schools: Convergence of Academics and Corporate expectations

(This Paper was presented at the International Conference On 'Global Competition and Brand Promotion' September 15-16, 2008, Institute of Public Enterprise, Osmania University, Hyderabad, Andhra Pradesh, India)

Lot of discussion has already taken place on the issue of professionalism in Management Education. In fact, it has already taken place and the debate now veers around the degree to which it should be pursued. One issue on which considerable convergence is already visible is that Management Education should be professional and in the hands of professional academicians. This takes this discussion to certain very contemporary and live issues. These issues are

1. Objectives of Management Education

2. Players in Management Education

3. Tools of Management Education

4. Faculty Profile in Management Education

5. Degree of importance to academic learning in Management Education

6. Research orientation in a B-School

7. Significance of Placement in the overall activity of Management Education

8. Institutes from India reaching out to foreign countries

9. Institutes in India facing competition from foreign Institutes spreading in India

OBJECTIVE OF MANAGEMENT EDUCATION:

Ever since Management Education has gained significance in India, this debate on its objective is going on. Education of any type is ultimately aimed at enlightening an individual in general spheres of life and later on in specific traits where his /her interests are identified by him/her as well as by his/her well-wishers. In the material sense of the word, most of us relate education as a means of acquiring a decent job which will create and nurture an identity for ourselves as well as our family members. With management education , this has become more obvious. In the decade of the 1990s, Management graduates from leading as well as not so known institutions started acquiring decent jobs which resulted in a good life both at home as well as workplace. This trend is continuing till now. Those who took advantage of this situation from 1990 onwards till mid 1990s, are themselves

parents now and see their ward as a future manager after themselves experiencing the advantages of this education. On the other side, those who have never been in this education hear about it and see the good life of such past and present graduates. This makes such class of people promote management education on these lines. All said and done, whether it is one or the other section along with the government bodies looking after the regulation of such education, it can be safely assumed as well as concluded that education in management discipline is basically directed towards acquiring a decent job in a good professional organization in the private sector as well as government sector, more in private sector. However, entrepreneurship through management education is also one of the objectives which has developed recently. As per AICTE, approval status of PGDM Institutions for 2007-2008 is as follows

Central Region-4, Eastern Region-13, Northern Region-37, North Western Region-40,Southern Region-18, South Western Region-11 and Western Region-25.

PLAYERS IN MANAGEMENT EDUCATION:

At present there are more than 900 management schools approved by AICTE,

majority of which lack adequate resources. There are various players in Management

Education and each has a definite role to play in furthering its cause. But, it is due to

lack of this expected role play which has led to many problems in making this

education as productive as it should have been. Although one can list many players,

major as well minor in the field, but according to me following are the major ones.

a. Government   b. Private Sector   c. Parents and Wards

Government:

Government has two roles to play in Management Education. One is that of a **regulator**

(AICTE) and the other is that of **running management education**. It has been doing both these

roles with considerable sincerity and it cannot be faulted for all the problems in this direction.

When it dons the role of a regulator, it faces lot of problems, not all of which are of its making. It

does not face much problem in regulating institutions run by itself because it will not point out

its own faults. **However, it is often seen that the problems come when government goes**

about regulating private institutions on a regular basis. The problems are mainly in the form

of lack of physical infrastructure, quality of teaching and support staff not up to the mark,

doubts in the public mind about recognition of the institute and perceived exploitation of parents

and students by managements of private institutes in the form of high-handed rules as well as

exorbitant fees, besides the placement commitments of these institutes not adhered to strictly. **As**

far as running its institutions are concerned, those institutions which are marked out as

autonomous run well and have created a distinct image in the mind of all involved. Either the government respects their autonomy or it involves only to the extent of disbursing grants and taking account of them at the most. In such institutions run by government in very autonomous manner , problems are not there and things move smoothly. On the other hand, where the autonomy is considerably less or non-existent, problems are a daily matter.

Private Sector:

Private Sector has made significant advances in Management

Education. There are Management Education institutions in the country

imparting education in the discipline at PG (MBA) level (This discussion

does not include UG courses in Management education run by same institutes or

institutes conducting only UG courses). Private sector involvement can be broadly

put in following categories

- Private sector controlled autonomous institutes not affiliated to any University and also not recognized by All India Council of Technical Education(AICTE) as well as not aided by University Grants Commission. .
- Private Sector controlled institutes affiliated to any University and recognized by All India Council of Technical Education(AICTE).

In such cases, many institutes have grown in size and stature through there consistent approach , quality of education, excellent Faculty and its regular development through regular training, strong emphasis on research of all types, appropriate infrastructure, excellent industry interface besides good placement record. Every Institute may not be good in each of these areas, but many are good in most of them. All those which are good in all areas are renowned all over the world. Problem arises when all the institutions which are good in very few of these requirements or none of these, but on the basis of good marketing, get students and anyhow claim to be among good institutions . They claim that they are good and try to convince their audiences(read parents and their children) about their claims anyhow. It is also important to mention here that those institutions which are actually good and maintain there standards as well as credentials continue to do so and not fall into a trap of complacency. This is a possibility when the private party behind an institution after seeing the institution rise in stature becomes complacent and starts taking things for granted and becomes indifferent towards academic growth. Such an institute will sooner or later fall out of reckoning of everyone. Institutions from Private Sector wedded to lofty ideals listed above regardless of there position in the education fraternity will command respect by all concerned. Such institutions should continue to maintain these credentials and remain in the reckoning forever.

Parents and Wards:

Parents who are concerned for a good management education for their children are at times a very harried lot. Specially those parents whose child has not been able to get to a government university MBA program or government university aided institute MBA Program or government university unaided institute MBA Program or even government aided autonomous institute program(PGDM or with some other name).After all these options are exhausted, then comes the host of unaided, unrecognized institutes/colleges which are not controlled by any body or council but are flourishing due to acceptance from the industry(mainly private sector). Some such institutes are not bad and they are very transparent in all their activities which is helpful to parents as well as their wards. Some institutes which are not having any transparency and try to bluff the parents and their wards in all aspects of management education are real problem group for the society. It is this menace that is making parents and wards doubt the over all spread of management education wherein otherwise good institutes are also clubbed with not so good ones. Parents and wards are not at fault if they do so as they are making judgments either on wrong information or no information at all. Sometimes, the problem lies with parents themselves. On the basis of a trend in favor of management education at PG level, they force/cajole their children to take it whereas a proper counseling would have revealed that their child would have been better placed in a different type of higher education. Children of such parents because of having no other option land in a management institute with half hearted interest and even if they anyhow complete the course, they still remain unfit for a managerial job. Some such students drop anyhow in between well before the course is over, either due to coping problem or their parents realize late there folly.

TOOLS OF MANAGEMENT EDUCATION:

Management Education has many tools which can be used to deliver the output to the audience (students). It is also important that along with the modern tools of management education , time tested tools are also maintained and used side by side. These tools can be as follows

- Chalk and black board (timeless tool)
- White board and Marker pen
- Over-head Projector
- LCD Projector

These tools are used in any other type of education but they come handy in management education at different points of time and depending upon the requirements of various courses in the management education. Over a period of time, all these tools have become handy in the discourse of management education in all types of management education institutions. However, there cannot be any best tool and different courses depending upon their diverse natures of handling by respective faculty members need a combination of these different tools in the best possible manner. The paramount role of the concerned faculty member cannot be ignored in this direction and faculty members have come up strongly in this direction.

FACULTY PROFILE IN MANAGEMENT EDUCATION:

This aspect has undergone tremendous developments in the phase post mid 1990s till now and it is still continuing with the unfinished churning which is good for all involved. The debate revolves around that faculty members in a management institute should or should not be pure academicians or pure professionals or a mix of both. Traditional school of thought says that academician in a true Indian sense has to be a *guru*(teacher) who imparts *gyan*(knowledge) to his/her *shishya*(student/disciple) without any expectation in return except guru-dakshina(parting goodies from the student at the end of the teaching). Moreover, this relationship of affection and respect for teacher continues for the whole life of the teacher as well as student. But, current higher education and in particular management education in India is in a completely different frame. The Faculty members as well as students besides promoters of management education have a uniform view that at the end of the course, students should be decently employable or self-employable with a heightened sense of responsibility towards the society at large. This is not a small responsibility which teachers are shouldering. The question arises as to who can be best fitted for this responsibility. Should he/she be complete academician preferably with a Ph.D or a smart corporate with considerable experience who can bring his/her experiences to class room and share it with budding management performers or a judicious mix of both ? In fact, the faculty profile should include a fair representation of all three types. There are ample reasons for this argument.

- A pure academician with a Ph.D has a research bent of mind and will orient students towards finding out new ways of management and its related developments besides making their academic foundations intact in the last phase of their class-room learning career.

- A smart corporate with considerable experience will be an asset due to vast contemporary industrial practices and can imbibe certain distinct traits in the students.

- A Faculty with a mix of academics as well as corporate experience will be useful in deciding where to share which experience depending upon the tempo of the classes as it moves with the course.

Over and above all this, a Faculty member in a Management Institute is also a mentor for students wherein he or she becomes a part of the student's life of 2 years in the institute and virtually hand-holds him or her in professional and personal life if required. Management Institutes which follow this general Faculty profile continue to maintain good standards as Faculty members , their backgrounds and their experience are the most crucial aspects of the respectability which the institute enjoys in public. However, there are institutes which do not adhere to one or more of these aspects and continue to remain either controversial or disrespectful in the public eye. The reasons for this controversy and disrespect can be attributed to promoters as well as to faculty members. Promoters with the motive of profit making at the core will anyhow run the institute by inducting anyone as faculty ignoring most of the essential requirement and also fudging documents in this regard for the regulators.

DEGREE OF IMPORTANCE TO ACADEMIC LEARNING IN MANAGEMENT EDUCATION:

It is often debated that students of Management education should or should not be emphasized academic learning .One side of the argument says that after all , it is a full fledged Post Graduate program and academic inputs should be heavy to give strong foundation to the student. The other side of the argument says that it being a professional course there should be more emphasis on practical orientation and less of academic or conceptual teaching. However, both the arguments hold good because it has to be a judicious mix and the proportions of this mix is the responsibility of this concerned faculty member who in turn is the right judge in deciding the proportion keeping in mind the conceptual as well as the practical development of the students. All said and done, at the end of the course, the students are expected to get well versed with concepts as well applications strongly embedded in their minds.

RESEARCH ORIENTATION IN A B- SCHOOL:

This is very important keeping in mind the nature of education imparted in a B-School. Continuous research , conceptual as well as empirical should be regularly on in the institute where-in faculty members along with students must be on the lookout for new and upcoming trends in management arena prevailing in the industry as well specific organizations (companies). The promoters of the institute have to keep in mind that this is good not only for the development of their faculty members but also for the over-all growth of the institute through regular development of knowledge products thereby bringing all-round respectability to the institute. The range pf knowledge products can be :

- Research article

- Conceptual paper

- Tailor made Corporate training program for specific company

- Consultancy assignments from time to time

Besides giving a strong research orientation to the institute, such activities become good revenue generating exercises whereby as per pre-decided proportion, revenue gets shared between faculty members and the institute. In other words, apart from academic development of all involved, incentives in decent monetary form motivate the entire system. Any institute where   this activity is lacking can be easily imagined as nothing more than a tutorial. So, although many institutes remain to serve as tutorials but some have gone beyond that and created a strong respectability among all involved.

SIGNIFICANCE OF PLACEMENT IN THE OVERALL ACTIVITY OF MANAGEMENT EDUCATION:

Placement is the most natural expectation of would be students who become students later on as well as their parents/guardians. Moreover, these placements have to be decent and there can be no denying this expectation. Now, some institutes claim hundred percent placements and make sure that it happens in a decent manner . On the other hand, some institutes claim but do not ensure it. This generates bickering, heartburns etc among student section. Other than these two types, some institutes claim hundred percent placement support but no placement guarantee. Here, the stakes are different and bickering, heartburns among the students are minimal as support outcomes depend upon the performance and merit of students involved. All said and done, placement support and its outcome add to the respectability and marketability of the institute, students as well as management education as a whole, but it has to be managed professionally. Continuous networking with the alumni makes this task easy and controllable. In other words, all involved have to make sure that the Institute does not become a placement agency. The irony is that a large number of institutes behave as placement agencies and in doing so academic environs suffer because out of four semesters, third semester onwards students interest take a completely different turn. This will never happen if the Institute strikes a balancing act and emphasize equal importance for academics as well as placements.

INSTITUTES FROM INDIA REACHING OUT TO FOREIGN COUNTRIES:

While keeping in mind all the above mentioned activities, many institutes and their promoters have started operations abroad and growing significantly in numbers as well as stature. Examples are IMT, BITs, S.P.Jain etc. These institutions have a strong brand presence in India and have worked to ensure that. In foreign context, there presence will be observed with respect to local institutes present there and the activities which they are doing. The profile of students in these institutes will be of following types

- Indians settled in those countries who see such institutes as a cultural link with their homeland

- Residents of the host country who have come up to realizing high standards of Indian institutes in India and interested in making their careers through them.

- Third country nationals who do not find good institutes in their countries as well as the host country   and look up to institutes coming from India.

- A mix of all the above population considering institutes from India as the only option left after trying and getting rejected for admissions from all over.

It is this last category mentioned above which Indian institutes abroad should be very careful as their rejections in other institutes may have happened mainly due to their own shortcomings in past academics etc. A thorough screening of this category may result in some otherwise bright students requiring a push to make a good life in future. Our B-Schools abroad should have that strong power of differentiation in as un-biased manner as possible.

INSTITUTES IN INDIA FACING COMPETITION FROM FOREIGN INSTITUTES SPREADING IN INDIA:

If we look at the institutions from abroad coming to India and establishing physical infrastructures to impart higher education in Management, then it is not much of a challenge for established Indian B-Schools. However, it has made these B-Schools tighten up their belts and they are not at all complacent about their exalted positions in the country. Challenge is more for not so established ones and which have come up in about last 2 decades i.e., 1990 onwards. Institutes in India growing in size and stature have to be careful of following things while competing with foreign institutes setting up operations in India

- A strong craving for foreign institutes with some sections of students and their parents on the basis of here-say or through experiences of their kith or kin. Some foreign institutes may be really genuine in all aspects and their intentions in setting off-shore center in India may also be genuine but it cannot be said for all institutes and universities.

- These foreign institutes/universities may not be having very stringent conditions and criteria for admissions and that may be the reason for many Indian students to feel attracted towards them.

- Marketing needs to be very professional on the part of Indian institutes where all the aspects from admission to the ultimate placements need to be highlighted with special emphasis on the strong academics to be pursued by aspiring students. It may involve highlighting tie-ups and accreditations with foreign institutes and bodies of repute. This highlighting may impact to the extent of admission of the students but beyond that real academics and their utility to the students need to be rigorously pursued to have a strong brand image. Moreover, now a days when every institute is having some or the other tie-up or accreditation, it is losing its sheen as a marketable tool for institutes.

References:

www.aicte.ernet.in

www.imt.edu

www.spjimr.org

Bajaj. K.K.(2001) 'Paradigm Shift in the Management of Colleges', University News, Vol. 39, no. 27, July 2-8, pp. 1-4 &8.

Chaudhari P.T. (1999) " Business Education – Indian and American   Scenario",   Indian Management, All India Management Association (AIMA) New Delhi, May 1999, pp.37.

Chaudhury N.R. (2001) "Management in Education" A.P.H Publishing Corporation New Delhi, pp. 17

De-Costa E.P.W. (2000) " Education : Foundation for Future", Edited article,   Monthly Public Opinion Survey, May-June 2000, pp.12.

Deetya (1996) "Higher Education Series, Occasional Paper No : 13",   Mapping the Futures : Local Culture, Routledge London, New York, pp. 169.

Dhankar R.S. (1998) "Long Summer in Management Education", Indian Management, AIMA, New Delhi, July 1998, pp. 51.

Ganguli P (1998) " Are Our Management Institutes Responsible Enough" Indian Management, AIMA, New Delhi, August, 1998; pp. 76-77.

Swain Dindayal and Sahu Suprava "Role Dynamics and Challenges for Management Education in India: A Vision for 2050", paper submitted at National Conference on 'Buiding Management Competences of India Inc' held at IBS Ahmedabad, Feb 24-25, 2005.

15. Management and Spiritualism: A Convergence of the two

(This Paper was presented at the Fourth Annual Education and Development Conference' during March 5-7, 2009, organized by Tomorrow People Organization, at Bangkok, Thailand)

It is a fact that Management is the art of getting things done through people tactfully. Another fact is Spiritualism which relates to soul and its consciousness. Experts in both fields are open to appreciate and criticize one another's area of operation, but all along this constant way of life there are a lot of similarities which make Management and Spiritualism complimentary to one another. I would like to make some observations from the point of view of a Faculty in Management Education which will make the convergence of Management and Spiritualism obvious. In doing so, I do not want to offend those who disagree with my observations.

My basic point is that one who is spiritual will be a good manager and on the other hand, one who is a good manager will continuously relate to consciousness of the soul which is spirituality. It never appears obvious but this is what I strongly feel exists in many of us. Another way of looking at it is the way in which we lead life. Instead of going into a very loaded discourse on life, I will put in very simple terms. Following are certain essentials of life which apply well to Management as well as spiritualism.

a. **Discipline**: This word which is the essence of life is a part of managing everything as well as having a strong role to play in making one spiritual. The intertwined nature of discipline is so obvious that one who practices it rigorously manages ones spiritual activities confidently. On the other hand a routine guided by the soul automatically makes ones management comfortable. We experience this whether we are at home or in our workplace. Even if we are at none of these two places, we pursue discipline while on vacation or at leisure.

b. **Ethics**: This issue is very debatable from every angle. Ethics emanate from morals which are very varied in all of us. What is ethical from one's point of view may be totally unethical from someone else's point of view. Vice-versa may also be possible. Now both of us swear by our souls in terming what is right and what is wrong according to both of us. Accordingly, we make our life move around these points of ethical and unethical behavior.

c. **Learning**: Each and every day in our life is spent in learning or unlearning something. This goes beyond the class room ambience and involves real experiences also. When it happens continuously, it does play a big role in moulding our spiritual beliefs at times(changing or re-enforcing). Similarly, we incorporate this learning in our day to day management of our routine. Now, here, belief (spiritual) as well as routine daily activity become intertwined with one another and keep on influencing one's personality on a regular basis.

d. **Perception**: Everyone of us possess the ability to perceive things, incidents etc according to our mind and its pace of work. Here our spiritual beliefs get enforced as well as contradicted at times. When we come across some incident or event which gels well with our spiritual thought process, our perception veers around it and becomes a learning with us to be shared with others. It almost becomes a scientific way of life with us and anything contrary to it, howsoever well documented and proved, will not get our attention and we will ignore it ultimately. We cannot blame our spiritual leanings for this activity but, we can.

see our conviction clearly about something which has been proved wrong scientifically.

d **Devotion**: This aspect is common to both spiritualism and management .A religious person in true sense is devoted to a cause and makes sure that in-spite of all odds, that cause is ensured in whatever frequency it is desired to be done. On the other hand, similar devotion is observed in a person wedded to management discipline. Every task is outlined on a daily, weekly or monthly basis and is given a priority accordingly. In exceptional circumstances, when due to some or the other reason, a task cannot be completed, its alternative or way out is identified and put in action. This gives satisfaction to a spiritualist as well as a manager that time has not gone to waste.

e. **Knowledge sharing**: It happens with the spiritualist that gains in knowledge is passed on to devotees or close circle through gatherings or informal get-togethers. Here the spiritualist is looked upon with respect and sought after for his /her learning by others. On the other hand, a manager who acquires hands on experience while working also becomes respected in the organization and his /her expert opinion/advice is sought after by colleagues as well as subordinates. However, there can be exceptions as every spiritualist and manager may not be that open to sharing knowledge.

f. **Shouldering Responsibility**: A spiritual person is never lacking in shouldering responsibility of his/her actions/deeds/teachings. I am not talking of those who masquerade as spiritual beings and dupe fellow humans and vanish at times when needed the most. Same can be said about a true manager. He/she takes complete responsibility of his/her actions and is ready to bear criticism for the same as he/she is ready for all appreciation consequent to his/her actions. Such a manager ultimately becomes a visionary and leader to his/her colleagues and subordinates. This goes true for a real spiritualist also who becomes a   savior   for his/her followers and makes every efforts in protecting and promoting his/her disciples.

f. **Minimizing errors in future**: Both the spiritualist as well as the manager make sure that they learn from all their actions. This helps them in identifying there errors and mistakes. Thereafter they make serious efforts in ensuring that these errors are not repeated in future. We may find many people who claim themselves as spiritualists or managers but keep on repeating the same mistakes. In literal sense they are neither spiritualists nor managers.

16. Competitive challenges to Marketing in an era of Generalization

(This Paper was presented at the International Conference on 'Global Economic Turbulences: Shifts in Business Structures and Systems' during July 12-14, 2009, organized by GITAM University, Rushikonda, Vishakhapatnam (Andhra Pradesh),India)

Marketing is all about competition. If not so, than what was marketing when there were monopolies or monopolistic tendencies. It is often said that it is competition which makes the significance of marketing more and more apt across the world and in all categories of products, services etc. The very presence of competition generates a challenge to all firms to excel in order to compete and in order to do so they have to differentiate with respect to other firms and their products and services. This requirement of differentiation generates activities, actions, reactions, events and what not by all companies involved in categories across the board. This whole mass of activities etc make marketing challenging as well as fascinating. All marketers who make sure that these activities are in control find themselves comfortably and challengingly poised. Others just don't exist as far as marketing is concerned. However, a very complex phenomenon seems to be happening in the recent times where differentiation and identity of companies in various categories of business appears blurred and generalization seems to be the buzzword everywhere. This has brought a very big burden on companies to create and maintain an identity. In fact, the very ability to compete becomes challenging, if not impossible. Certain points need to be elaborated in this regard.

a. **Identity of companies**: There used to be times when companies were known for a particular type or category of products and services and nothing more or less than that. Besides that, these companies zealously guarded their operating turfs and made all efforts to make sure that they are always recognized for these turfs. Even if new products or services were brought out by companies, these did not go out of the broad ambit of their identities. But times have changed considerably and now companies are not zealously guarding their identities as far as the specializations in products /services are concerned. They are going out of their ways in ensuring everything to everyone. For example, in Communication services, a company may have started operation as a mobile service provider in a specialized technology but it has come a long way now by offering mobile service in another technology, adding to it land line telephony also and further capping it with providing service for dish television. Similarly, a company known earlier for providing main frames and servers extending into providing desktops in computers, adding laptops in its portfolio and further projecting itself as providing total Information Technology solutions. The list is endless and a whole volume of literature can be readied in this direction. Many times, within the companies, such decisions look very logical as these do not dilute the identity of the company but only enlarge it. However, from the customer/consumer perspective, it looks confusing and multiple interpretations start unfolding in the market. Companies are always not successful in controlling or minimizing the negative spread of this interpretation.

b. **Competitive pressure**: At times, it also happens that a particular competitor or a number of competitors start taking actions and

decisions which forces a company to do a rethinking as far as its identity is concerned. It requires examining the word competition as such. Traditionally , competition implied a company or companies making products or providing services or a combination of both similar to the other company. But the word competition has acquired a very different perspective. How can a company making Air Conditioners compete with a company providing Travel and Tour services? But, it can happen. One advertisement of an Air-conditioner tried to project an enjoyable hot summers with a good AC instead of looking forward to travel to cool destinations. If consumers really start taking these communications seriously, and club it with growing concern for security related to leisure travel in many of us, an AC communication can make a dent in the market of a tour operator. There are numerous examples where the competition has gone beyond traditional product and service categories. Optimism may rubbish it, but a challenge can emerge out of it. Here, the challenge is to face it and overcome the challenge than to lament on the collapse of traditional aspect of competition.

c. **Pressure of Consumer behavior**: Consumer behavior is the essence of any marketing activity from time to time. Consumers drive the companies to perform in myriad ways thereby motivating them to meet as well as surpass their benchmarks. Any company which ignores consumer buying behavior will cease to exist eventually. But, this never happens as every professional and alert organization gives utmost credence to measuring and monitoring consumer behavior regularly in order to keep pace with times and remain relevant always. Inspite of this alertness, even the best of professional organizations and companies face stiff challenges due to changes in consumer behavior patterns for which reasons are not always comprehensible. Numerous examples can be cited in this direction. Traditionally speaking, real estate, retail banking, stock market, life insurance, mutual funds appear to be having focused objective and companies offering such services are right in assuming their very different identities. But, if we look at the trends in the second half of the decade 2000-2009, due to recessionary trends, certain consumers have gone to the extent of withdrawing whatever is left in their kitty of stocks and shares after facing a severe loss and putting remaining amount not only in bank fixed deposits but that too in certain nationalized banks. Did any stock broking or share broking firm or agent ever considered a bank fixed deposit as a competitive product ? No. But, the whole of the year 2008 actually forced them to start thinking in this direction. So much so, that many private sector banks which looked down upon fixed deposits as old fashioned non marketable products and services competed vehemently and are still competing with one another in marketing their fixed deposits at attractive rates. Examples can be screened out from various sectors. All boils down to the consumer and the behavior which the consumer shows. Many of us as consumers have started giving importance to safety aspects along with risk taking attitude. Another facet holds importance here. Awareness level of consumers has undergone a sea change since long and we are not at all ignorant whether we are highly educated or not. The revolution in information technology, access of any information at any point of time and ever increasing consciousness of consumers about the right and wrong as to what they buy or not buy has made it ever challenging for companies to promote anything and everything. It may not be an exaggeration to say that consumer behavior at times itself has become a competition to companies market expansion and no company in the world can override it. Otherwise what is the reason for cosmetics companies to emphasize the health aspects of their various products more than anything else which was not the case before the information revolution began. Another important development since mid 1990s has been the ever increasing purchasing power of consumers clubbed with the ever increasing availability of loans for home, car and other personal possessions. There used to be times when individuals and families decided on certain major purchases (read luxury) after accumulating a certain level of money and when basic purchase have already been done as either loan providers were not available or these were not institutionalized or having a loan was not considered as a good sign in society. Now a days, having a loan is a fashion and it is not at all wrong to have at least two loans running at a time. This has made families of all classes acquire anything at a very early age and not to wait for money to come and then purchase heavy items. Moreover, the difference between economy and luxury purchases is very difficult to understand as everything is available on loan or EMI. Any one can buy any car, go on a star cruise and fly on any flight across the world.

d. **Product identities getting blurred**: Certain product categories have lost there identities leading to a very difficult situation wherein either one or the other product has vanished from the market or has become a part of some other product. It has resulted in a challenge to not only identity but the degree of competition between products. A mobile phone is having a watch, digital diary, calendar, calculator, currency converter, audio music player, video player, camera (still as well as video), computer as well as television all rolled into one and the more sophisticated a mobile handset is, the more features and characteristics it will possess. Now, how many of us look at our wristwatch to know the time ? In fact, how many of us put on a wristwatch to keep track of the time ? . Should this not affect the marketing strategy of a company like Titan ? There may be numerous   questions related to various products listed above which there manufacturers and marketers have to answer to define and redefine there businesses and keep up with times.

e. **International company presence in India**: Domestic Indian organizations have played a significant role in raising the benchmark for Indian corporates to improve, excel and face foreign companies head on. However, every company coming from every country was not taken seriously by Indian companies. A lot has been said and written about products in every category coming from China and challenging established India companies on the base of their extremely low pricing at the retail level .Almost since late 1990s, our Indian companies and their important decision makers have rejected this Chinese challenge on the ground of the inferior quality put forward by Chinese manufacturers and to a considerable extent Indian customers/consumers have accepted that. But since mid 2000s onwards, Chinese companies have started communicating seriously about their quality along with a low price. If this communication acquires acceptability over a period of time, all major and minor Indian companies in all product categories across the board will have a tough time unless and until they do not rework their price-quality equation and subsequent communication.

References:

www.yahoo.com

www.yahoo.co.in

www.indiatimes.com

www.rediffmail.com

www.titan.com

Kotler Philip., Keller Kevin., Koshy Abraham., and Jha Mithileshwar, *Marketing Management-A South Asian Prespective* 13e 2009, Pearson Education

Cteora Philip R., Grasham John L., and Salwan Prashant, International Marketing,13 e 2008, New Delhi: Tata Mc-Graw Hill Publishing Company Limited.

17. Changing Dimensions of Global Marketing

(This Paper was presented at the Second Nitte International Conference on 'Redefining the Roles of Business, NGOs, and Governments: A Mission for a Better Global Society' at Justice K. S. Hegde Institute of Management, NITTE-574110, near Mangalore, during December 29-30, 2010)

Every company in this world is a part of marketing as the era of monopolies has literally ended . Even in cases of some monopoly organizations in this world, marketing for the cause of social responsibility is done to ensure the respectability for the company wherever it is operating. Many companies across the world are having global presence and expanding in that arena. Some companies which are not global aspire to be global and continue to do activities in that direction. Some other companies which are neither globally present nor have any aspiration to be like that get affected by global companies in their domestic geographic areas of operations. In other words, exposure to global marketing exercises is common phenomenon for many companies and it becomes essential for every company to learn global marketing practices and the changing dimensions which it brings from time to time. It has implications in many aspects of marketing. Some are discussed here.

a. **Product Development**. It is an area which is challenging as well as rewarding to companies in global marketing provided the companies are willing to take risks and show patience continuously.   A company may be oriented locally or globally, but it is reaching the whole world slowly and gradually. This makes it very important for companies to adapt themselves globally with respect to their products. This adaptation may be cultural, legal, social, technical, ethical and any other dimension/s essential for specific markets. All these aspects require adaptation because product usage in different countries and markets requires adaptation. Many times a market dictates a completely new use to an old product which is not at all relevant in other markets of the product. At other times, a market dictates a new product to a company which may not have any relevance to other markets. Sometimes, a minor modification in design, shape and other features of the product results in big satisfaction for an existing market.

b. **Customer Satisfaction**. Every company across the world makes every effort to ensure customer satisfaction in order to compete effectively and improve continuously. With Global Marketing coming of age, ensuring customer satisfaction and continuously striving for the same has become the order of the day. Sometimes it requires complex decisions to be taken at the Corporate Headquarter level and at times, it can be managed at the local market level. This expectation of satisfaction on the part of the consumer is ever increasing and any company world-over has to factor this aspect regularly. Moreover, a company which keeps on delivering on this front is expected to do the same continuously as compared to other companies which are not always meeting customer satisfaction requirements. Customer satisfaction has always been a very dynamic and unpredictable aspect in the marketing strategy of the company. However, it is important and it can be impacted by numerous things within as well as outside the control of the companies. Companies have to continuously make efforts to ensure that controllable factors are exploited to the fullest thereby making customer satisfaction a continuous exercise through company offerings and uncontrollable factors are either not touched or their impact does not become a problem in any way. Customer satisfaction and its degree continuously gets affected by the social, cultural, political, legal and various other aspects/factors which surround customers and which give a dynamic identity to customers. At times, certain factors become more obvious than others and at times certain other factors acquire the same or more significance. Marketers have to be very careful in determining the dominance of different factors at different times and tailoring their strategies accordingly.

c. **Delivery**: The access which the customer has to the product/ service of his/her liking makes a big impact on the success of the same. Whether it is the typical small store in every market or the specialized retail outlet or through online mode, the ease of acquiring the product/service makes the customer strongly loyal to it. Whenever this access comes into trouble for whatever reasons, customer/s feel surprised and when this surprise becomes frequent, it generates negative attitudes towards the same products/services which otherwise are liked very much. Companies have to make sure that the accessibility of their offerings is never a problem and supplies are maintained so that retail points and other points of delivery are rarely short of supply.

d. **Communication**: It is very important as far as global marketing is concerned. When communication for domestic marketing is challenging, it becomes more challenging as far as global marketing is concerned. However, it can be planned to suit the company purpose. Marketing communication has lot of tools to make the markets informed in various ways. It needs to be constantly identified which tool/s will work at what time and which not. Different geographic markets will not respond to various tools in a similar manner. Indian market scenario has demonstrated this to a large number of foreign originating companies which have entered India and made their presence felt here. Although Indian market and consumer is dynamic and constantly experimenting with new products and ideas, but companies cannot take them for granted as far as their cultural and social norms are concerned, thereby communicating with them carefully. Where ever, Indian consumer has felt that its feelings or emotions were hurt by company communications, it has responded in its own way and made such companies realize it fast to apply changes in its communications. This also holds good for Indian companies doing business and communicating with customers outside India . Communication should make people feel closer towards company offerings and if that is not happening, it should at least not offend their feelings. At times, it happens that certain sections of consumers either get hurt or the message goes wrongly to them and it results in partial or complete rejection of the product/service by them. Although it could have happened by mistake also, but the onus of solving this perceived or real communication problem lies with the company and/or its communication agency. It acquires additional importance in global marketing as cultural barriers need to be bridged here and it is not easy to do the same. Either in the name of protection to local culture or as per host country laws , the firm has to encounter more than one barriers to its communications and these serve as challenges as well as opportunities to the firm in a new geographic area.

e. **Ethical Conduct**: It is very crucial for companies operating globally to keep in mind there conduct which should not lend them in any unwarranted controversy. In the first place itself, any foreign company is looked at with suspicion world over. It makes it doubly important for a global player to ensure ethical conduct in foreign locations with respect to any aspect of its operations like pricing, cultural sensitivity, local tastes and preferences, employee management and motivation etc. Due to certain big brands across the world found involved in unethical practices from time to time, the country of origin and other possible companies from the same country acquire bad name by default thereby making it very challenging for them to come out of this bracket. Names like Enron, Arther Anderson, Satyam etc have made this challenge increase manifold. One very important aspect in this direction is the already established brand image of the company in other parts of the world which makes it complacent and overconfident at the time of entering a new geographic area. It literally replicates here its strategies in other geographies taking the new geography for granted. Rarely this has worked and it will rarely work in future. As a result of this complacent and overconfident approach, the company goes into problems on multiple ethical fronts and finds it difficult to come out of it. By the time, it comes out of this controversy, crucial time gets lost and the damage already gets done. International Marketing Research and its institutionalization in the company is not only the solution but an essential aspect of the company operations for all times.

f. **Strategic Alliances**: Alliances which come up as part of various strategies designed by companies to gain access to global markets serving the purpose of all stakeholders serve the interests of companies very well. But these need to be carried out with caution and after due research. A particular company in a market or geographical area may have acquired a name which might be dubious and will only damage the company which allies with it. On the other hand, the laws within a country may require a company entering it to have some form of an alliance with a domestic player as a stake holder, major, minor, or equal. Even if this requirement is not there and a foreign player can go ahead with 100% FDI, it makes sense at times to have an alliance for some time to gain a hold in the market and subsequently come out of it at a later stage without any acrimony. Even then, we find certain alliances continuing although the FDI rules get changed because the foreign player realizes that it is better to have a partner/ally in the host country than going independent .

g. **Level of Market Development**: It is very important to identify the synergy between all the above aspects which will indicate the level to which the market in a particular country or countries has developed. In some cases product development can experimented, and in some other cases strategic alliances will have more acceptability, and in some further cases ethical conduct may be more important as compared to other aspects. It will be a huge variety of information from all over the world and in order to realize and interpret it regularly for the company advantage, a robust International Marketing Research will always be required. International Marketing Research is the most important activity for any company having global ambitions and it needs to be done regularly with utmost professionalism.

Conclusion: It can be inferred from the above discussion that global marketing has multiple parameters on which decisions have to be taken and all these parameters have become very dynamic in this rapidly dynamic and competitive world. The parameters continuously play roles in different intensities and durations and most of the times are characterized by their unpredictability. Global Marketing efforts have to give importance to continuous marketing research so that this unpredictability can be brought in control at appropriate times on a continuous basis.

References:

www.google.com

www.worldbank.org

www.imf.org

www.business.com

www.globaledge.msu.edu

www.oecd.org

www.disney.go.com

Kotler Philip., Keller Kevin., Koshy Abraham., and Jha Mithileshwar, *Marketing Management-A South Asian Prespective* 13e 2009, Pearson Education

Cteora Philip R., Grasham John L., and Salwan Prashant, *International Marketing,* 13 e 2008, New Delhi: Tata Mc-Graw Hill Publishing Company Limited.

Belch George E., Belch Michael A., and Purani Keyoor, *Advertising and Promotion-An Integrated Marketing Communications Perspective* 7 e (SIE) 2010, Tata Mc-Graw Hill Education Private Ltd, New Delhi.

Daniels John D, Radebaugh Lee H, Sulivan Daniel P , and Salwan Prashant, *International Business-Environments and Operations* 12 e 2010, Pearson Education

18. Challenges to Indian Retail Marketing with FDI in Retailing a reality: 2012 and beyond

(This Paper was presented at the International Seminar on "Neoteric Trends in Functional Management" ISNTFM-2013 March 23-24, 2013,organized by Faculty of Management Studies(FMS), Janardhan Rai Nagar Rajasthan Vidyapeeth (D) University, Udaipur (Rajasthan), India)

Retailing has got revolutionized in India since early 1990s with the onset of liberalization and related reforms from time to time. However, the rapidity with which it took its different forms and formats in the first decade of the 21st century(2001-2010) have taken many by surprise. In the beginning, it was felt apprehensively that kirana stores will become extinct once the big retail format owned and controlled by Indian Corporate houses become operative. However, in the period 1995 and onwards, it is for everyone to see that not only kirana stores have remained there but expanded and new ones have come up alongside. They have become more organized and competitive and in fact grown with the coming and growth of organized big retailing. On the other hand, big organized retailing has also benefitted as they learned and incorporated personalized selling techniques so common with decades old kirana stores which are a part and parcel of our lives since our childhood. In a way it has been and still is a win-win situation for those players who believe in competition and working hard to get the best out of it. For others, common argument is that kirana vs organized big retailing finishing kirana stores all over the country. The argument goes on and every player in this argument rattles figures and statistics to support its argument. From an academic angle, this debate is important as it is going to transform our country at the end of the second decade of the 21st century (2011-2020). It can be elaborated on the basis of following points

a. **Consumer benefit:** The biggest benefit to the consumers across India is the variety in price, offerings, ease of shopping, and a completely vibrant atmosphere where shopping is fun most of the time and not a boring or mundane chore as was the case earlier. Apart from that, with everything operated as part of a sequence from the point of entry to exit from a store makes consumers feel comfortable even after going for bulk buying which is normally the case in organized retail shopping. In all these benefits derived by consumers, the price discounts or any other form of cash based benefit related to the price of purchases is by far the biggest benefit which I feel is nothing less than a revolution which was not there earlier. In fact, it is taken as a learning by small kirana store to be offered to its consumers. These small kirana operators are also applying many tactics to make consumers comfortable like big organized retailing.

b. **Small Kirana Store benefit:** There are numerous benefits derived by small kirana stores ever since big organized retailing has come to stay in our country. It is in the form of store layout, better care for the customers, more variety being stocked, home delivery service, additional discounts etc. Moreover, small kirana stores have also learnt the art of better display within their limited premises to match as much as possible the orderliness as well as cleanliness demonstrated by big organized retailing. Another benefit observed is the increase of store space by kirana stores in many locations by buying the adjacent shop or putting better use of the existing space.

c. **Organized Big Retail benefit:** Here the benefits are numerous and not limited. One of the foremost benefit is to operate in a market which is having the second highest population in the world after China. Moreover, the purchasing power of this ever increasing population is rising rapidly and bulk buying concept within them is catching fast across the country. So the volumes exist and will continue to not only exist but grow . Keeping in mind these ever increasing volumes across the country, big retailers have come up with various forms and formats of retail offerings which go from exclusive branded retail outlet on the one hand and a store in a store concept on the other hand and a host of different combinations in between making customers come across choices unheard of till as late as 1990s.

d. **Benefit to farmers and other suppliers:** This is specially relevant when big organized retailing sells farm fresh produce as well as processed food requiring farm inputs. The organized retail players normally enter into contracts and other legal procedures to ensure regular supplies from farmers as per their requirements as well as to the benefit of farmers. Moreover, with advance planning aspects in play, regular and big orders are given to farmers which results in big money also coming to them, and at the same time all logistics and transportation related work is taken care of by big retail players. The farmers benefit from this arrangement as they get a very high price from their buyers besides huge regular orders and they need not market much as once they meet expected quality standards of these big retail players, orders remain for long times to come. As compared to these benefits, farmers have to struggle a lot, haggle for a fair price, as well as to do lot of marketing, besides undertake long arduous journeys to nearby mandis/haats, etc when they deal with middlemen or other agents or even with consumers ,who buy from them. A sizeable quantity regularly bought by big retail players helps farmers organize their farm activity as they become a part of full fledged and robust supply chain of organized retail industry. If organized retail keeps on growing like this and expands, farmers will become more a part of organized supply chain networks across the country and will not be left alone to handle climatic problems related to dependence on rains, etc for maximizing their produce.

It is argued that with the setting up and growth of foreign owned organized retailing in India, small kirana stores will get wiped off. The same argument was put forward by certain sections of corporate world ,society and political spectrum when Indian owned organized retailing was being decided upon and proposed in late 1980s and early 1990s. However, it is now over two decades since when it all started and is increasing by the day. At the same time, small kirana stores have not only remained, but have also increased in numbers as well as have become very competitive with times. The argument in favor of FDI in retailing is that when small kirana stores can work their way and stand as well as emerge better with competition from Indian owned organized retailing, they can very well do the same with respect to FDI in organized retailing. However, whatever is the argument, the road to FDI in retailing is there and the players have to travel on this road as there is no question of any return on this issue.

Study

A study was conducted in Ahmedabad wherein Ten players were asked a set of following questions related to the above topic. These ten players consisted of five Big organized retailers and five kirana stores spread across the city of Ahmedabad. The questionnaire addressed to these players is as follows.

Questionnaire for Big Organized Retailers

1. Entry of FDI in retailing in India will hurt/harm your business

   a. Yes   b. No

2. Consumer will be benefited from FDI in retailing in India

   a. Yes   b. No

3. You will learn from them to compete better

   a. Yes   b. No

4. Farmers and Suppliers will be benefitted from FDI in retailing in India

   a. Yes   b. No

5. Any other opinion which you would like to share with us

Questionnaire for Kirana Stores

1. Entry of FDI in retailing in India will hurt/harm your business

   a. Yes   b. No

2. Consumer will be benefited from FDI in retailing in India

   a. Yes   b. No

3. You will learn from them to compete better

    a. Yes   b. No

4.   Farmers and Suppliers will be benefitted from FDI in retailing in India

    a. Yes   b. No

5. Any other opinion which you would like to share with us

In fact, same questionnaire was addressed to both the categories of players as I have *assumed* that issues facing both of them are similar, if not completely identical. The outcome of the survey is tabled as follows.

Big Organized Retailers Survey summary

1. Entry of FDI in retailing in India will hurt/harm your business

    a. Yes   3 b. No 2

2. Consumer will be benefited from FDI in retailing in India

    a. Yes 5 b. No 0

3. You will learn from them to compete better

    a. Yes   3 b. No 2

4.   Farmers and Suppliers will be benefitted from FDI in retailing in India

    a. Yes   3 b. No 2

5. Any other opinion which you would like to share with us

    a. India is not a country where FDI is retail is required.It will affect small business and retailers

       very badly.

    b. If FDI will come then hard earned money of Indians will go out.

c. It will affect our business &all retailers will be really badly affected. Also that will ruin the

Indian Firms

d. Job opportunity will increase, benefit to customer as they will get more options and also

goods of international standard, no chance of cheating like adulteration or mixing by this

store

e. We will get new standards to compete

Kirana Stores Survey summary

1. Entry of FDI in retailing in India will hurt/harm your business

    a. Yes   2 b. No 3

2. Consumer will be benefited from FDI in retailing in India

    a. Yes   4 b. No 1

3. You will learn from them to compete better

    a. Yes   1 b. No 4

4. Farmers and Suppliers will be benefitted from FDI in retailing in India

    a. Yes 2 b. No 3

5. Any other opinion which you would like to share with us

    1. According to me, we should not protest. Because money will help develop our country and

    goodwill of my business will not let them takeover our business. It is going to help our country

    anyhow

    2. No Opinion

3. No Opinion

4. No benefit to farmers as though middle man would be eliminated they will buy goods at low

   rates only. People won't go to malls for small, daily requirements, so no harm to retailers

5. No Opinion

From the above small but pointed survey based on the questionnaire cited before it, certain points are clear from the angle of big retailers.

1. 60% of big retailers feel that entry of FDI in retail will hurt/harm their business.

2. 100% of big retailers feel that consumer will be benefited from FDI in retailing in India.

3. 60% of big retailers feel that they will learn from FDI players to compete better.

4. 60% of big retailers feel that farmers and suppliers will be benefitted from FDI in retailing in India

5. Five big retailers have the following subjective opinions

    a. India is not a country where FDI is retail is required.It will affect small business and retailers

       very badly.

    b. If FDI will come then hard earned money of Indians will go out.

    c. It will affect our business & all retailers will be really badly affected. Also that will ruin the

       Indian Firms

    d. Job opportunity will increase, benefit to customer as they will get more options and also

       goods of international standard, no chance of cheating like adulteration or mixing by this

       store

e. We will get new standards to compete

From the above small but pointed survey based on the questionnaire cited before it, certain points are clear from the angle of kirana stores.

1. 40% of kirana stores feel that entry of FDI in retail will hurt/harm their business.

2. 80% of kirana stores feel that consumer will be benefited from FDI in retailing in India.

3. 20% of kirana stores feel that they will learn from FDI players to compete better.

4. 40 % of kirana stores feel that farmers and suppliers will be benefitted from FDI in retailing in India

5. Five kirana stores have the following subjective opinions

    a. According to me, we should not protest. Because money will help develop our country and goodwill of my business will not let them takeover our business. It is going to help our country anyhow

    b. No Opinion

    c. No Opinion

    d. No benefit to farmers as though middle man would be eliminated they will buy goods at low rates only. People won't go to malls for small, daily requirements, so no harm to retailers

    e. No Opinion

Conclusion

Following things can be fairly concluded from the above non-empirical case study

1.   60% of big retailers feel that entry of FDI in retail will hurt/harm their business.

2.   100% of big retailers feel that consumer will be benefited from FDI in retailing in India.

3.   60% of big retailers feel that they will learn from FDI players to compete better.

4.   60% of big retailers feel that farmers and suppliers will be benefitted from FDI in retailing in India.

5.   40% of kirana stores feel that entry of FDI in retail will hurt/harm their business.

6.   80% of kirana stores feel that consumer will be benefited from FDI in retailing in India.

7.   20% of kirana stores feel that they will learn from FDI players to compete better.

8.   40 % of kirana stores feel that farmers and suppliers will be benefitted from FDI in retailing in India

9   Big retailers have diverse subjective views on FDI in retailing which included bad effect of FDI on small business and retailers, Indian money going out of the country, increased job opportunity, and better standards of competition.

9.   Kirana Stores did not give much subjective opinion except that they felt that their business will not get affected due to their goodwill , customers will not go to big retailers for daily purchases, and farmers will not get much benefit as big retailers will anyhow purchase from them at less price.

References

www.google.com

www.worldbank.org

www.imf.org

www.business.com

www.globaledge.msu.edu

www.oecd.org

www.disney.go.com

Kotler Philip., Keller Kevin., Koshy Abraham., and Jha Mithileshwar, *Marketing Management- A South Asian Prespective* 14 e 2013, Pearson Education

Cteora Philip R., Grasham John L., and Salwan Prashant, *International Marketing,* 13 e 2008, New Delhi: Tata Mc-Graw Hill Publishing Company Limited.

Belch George E., Belch Michael A., and Purani Keyoor, *Advertising and Promotion-An Integrated Marketing Communications Perspective* 7 e (SIE) 2010, Tata Mc-Graw Hill Education Private Ltd, New Delhi.

Daniels John D, Radebaugh Lee H, Sulivan Daniel P , and Salwan Prashant, *International Business-Environments and Operations* 12 e 2010, Pearson Education

Research support:

Avinash Ahuja, Student, MBA-2011-13 Sem III, B.K School of Business Management, Gujarat University, Ahmedabad.

Manali Dalal, Student, MBA-2011-13 Sem III, B.K School of Business Management, Gujarat University, Ahmedabad.

19.   Marketing of Services: Challenges and opportunities with respect to demographic dividend in India

(This Paper was presented at the National Conference on Emerging Trends in Management Research, 27th to 28th November 2015,organized by Narsee Monjee Institute of Management Studies (NMIMS), Hyderabad (India))

Introduction

It is often said that India is a happening country as far as demographic dividend is concerned. Demographic dividend implies a large number of consuming people for all types of products and services belonging to all ages, both sexes, spread geographically across the country and practicing various professions etc. Such a dynamic population is a strong market and will remain a market for companies of all types of products and services. In the current decade, the young population of India is constantly giving huge and ever increasing numbers to service providers of all types eg., mobile phones, food and beverages, entertainment, higher education etc.

Going by statistics of various sources.

If we go by the reports of The International Labour Organisation (ILO), by 2020, India will have 116 million workers in the work-starting age bracket of 20 to 24 years, as compared to China's 94 million. Most of this population will be very young with working energies on their sides for long times to come. It clearly gets reflected in estimations projecting the average age in India by the year 2020 as 29 years as against 40 years in the USA, 46 years in Europe and 47 years in Japan. Going deep into the research, it highlights that . By 2035 , i.e., in around 20 years the labour force in the industrialized world will decline by 4%, in China by 5%, while in India it will increase by 32%. To add more to the statistics, IMF reported in 2011 that India's demographic dividend has the potential to add 2 percentage points per annum to India's per capita GDP growth over the next two decades.

Is this demographic dividend realized or not?

This demographic dividend is the advantage that will accrue to India being blessed with a young population in the first half of the 21st century . However, it all will depend on whether we can educate and train it to take advantage of the opportunities that the 21st century world offers. Self-realized individuals are an asset to themselves as well as for corporations and organizations making and providing all type of products and services. This self-realization comes through education which has emerged as the most significant instrument of individual self-realization and democratic empowerment in our times. It requires companies to participate in this education of masses of people over and above their conventional education which masses take throughout their life. Company based education relates to making the masses understand the utility and value of their company's offerings in the lives of the consumers. This dynamic experiential knowledge coupled with conventional education through educational institutions at primary, higher secondary, as well as higher education level will help all stakeholders take full advantage of this demographic dividend which India is experiencing and is expected to experience for decades to come. In the 21st century, knowledge, and the instrument of its spread, education, will increasingly become the prime determinants of the success and worth of any nation or civilization, through its people, education institutions, social bodies, as well as organizations in business.

India after 1980s

 Since early 1990s, the meaning of success in this country has also undergone a paradigm shift. Prior to 1991, India was often referred to through the metaphor of the elephant, an animal whose association with our nation had less to do with local zoology and more with the perception of both the country and the animal as lumbering, ponderous, slow to move and slower to change. This simile or analogy was owing to India's seemingly lethargic pace of economic and social progress, anaemic policy reforms, and the modest dreams of its population for change, which were made worse by the weight of its own burgeoning population. 1990s showed that the metaphor had begun to outlive its already limited utility when a major change rendered it practically irrelevant.

1991 proved to be a watershed moment when, in a spectacular break from past practice, India undertook a dramatic transformation through economic liberalization. Declaring that "no power on earth can stop an idea whose time has come," then Finance Minister Dr Manmohan Singh launched a slew of economic policy reforms that launched and propelled India into an increasingly globalising world. The economic reforms which included conscious liberalization, measured privatization, and increasing globalization of the country's economy -- opened a wonderland of opportunities for India. The following two decades of of impressive growth, averaging nearly 8%, followed. Although favorable demographics and the enormous economic opportunities are available in the globalizing world, but education remains the most important tool for realizing the full potential of our youthful nation. It can be safely said that basic education is a prerequisite to empower each individual in the quest to pursue these economic opportunities. Books are the best friends for this demographic dividend and corporates will be better off If books are always with this youth. In fact, companies can campaign vigorously to promote the culture of reading and learning to the vast youth population on the rise. It will help in transforming the collective energy of our youngsters into mature ideas, well-developed skills, and a sense of confidence, hope and capability. All this will lead to ever dynamic market for companies. This requires taking head-on the key challenges plaguing Indian education and vocational training. It will not only help corporates in having dynamic consumers for their goods and services but our own people will become the workhorse of the world, as other countries' ageing populations turn to us for the provision of goods and services. If we fail to do so, it will be a demographic disaster, since unemployed, frustrated and unemployable young men become prey to the blandishments of extremists and fanatics, as we have already seen in a number of insurgencies, particularly in our educationally under-served tribal areas. The spread and expanse of Maoism or Naxalism in about 165 of our 625 districts, exploit the available pool of young men without education, unemployable as well as unemployed, who have no stake in our society because we have not equipped them with the education or skills to take advantage of the 21st century economy. It justifies good, effective and relevant education and skill development not only as a social and economic necessity but a natural security imperative for India. Moreover, any government at the center or in various states need not do politics on this issue as it is completely apolitical.

Economic development of a nation gets reflected by the percentage of people in that country employed in services sector or tertiary sector jobs . This shift from primary and secondary activities to tertiary activities by the citizens of a country reflects that it is on the path of progress. Over 60% of contribution to gross domestic product (GDP) in India comes from India's services sector. It has matured considerably during the last few years.

Information Technology (IT) and IT enabled Services (ITeS) sectors as well as e-commerce and its growth in India has led to a significant growth in the services sector. This sector in India comprises a wide range of activities such as transportation, logistics, financial, business process outsourcing services, healthcare, trading, and consultancies, among many others. Moreover, with the Government of India's liberal foreign direct investment (FDI) policies, the services sector has attracted the highest amount of foreign equity among all other sectors in the Indian economy.

Market Size

The Indian services sector has attracted the highest amount of FDI equity inflows in the period April 2000-September 2014, amounting to about US$ 40,684.98 million which is about 18 per cent of the total foreign inflows, according to the Department of Industrial Policy and Promotion (DIPP). The HSBC Purchasing Managers Index (PMI) for services stood at 52.2 points in July 2014, expanding for the third month in a row. As per the data provided by International Data Corporation (IDC), the total mobile services market revenue in India is expected to touch US$ 37 billion in 2017 growing at a compound annual growth rate (CAGR) of 5.2 percent. Apart from that ,the growth in the ITeS sector has resulted in increasing competition between the different brands in the e-commerce sector. Due to this, it is expected that the e-commerce sector will generate close to 150,000 jobs within the next 2-3 years. According to Mr R Dinesh, Chairman, CII Institute of Logistics Advisory Council and Joint Managing Director, TVS Sons Ltd, the logistics sector in India valued at US$ 101 billion in 2013 is expected to grow by 10 per cent per annum to reach US$ 136 billion by 2016.

Investments

Big investments by companies in the services sector in the recent past is a strong point to be noted. Some of these are as follows

a. George Soros-backed Aspada Investment Co has invested US$ 2 million in New Delhi-based Allfresh Supply Management. Allfresh, a B2B business, operates across the entire fresh fruit value chain from farm extension services for small-hold farmers to postharvest controlled atmosphere supply.

b. Zomato has acquired Gastronauci, a Poland-based restaurant search service. It is Zomato's fourth acquisition in three months making Zomato's presence now in 16 countries, and provides information for over 260,000 restaurants in these nations.

c. The aquisition of the cash management business of Danish major ISS by SIS Prosegur for about Rs 150 crore (US$ 24.25 million) making it India's second largest cash management operator. SIS Prosegur operates in 320 cities across the country.

d. Deutsche Post DHL plans to test its e-commerce business model for the Asia-Pacific region in India and will invest more than €100 million (US$ 124.84 million) in the country over the next two years to create infrastructure for itself.

e. Signing of a five-year contract by Ramco Systems Ltd with the Asia division of Netherlands-based Koninklijke Vopak NV to integrate a part of its regional human resource functions into a single platform. Ramco's services will now be made available to over 700 Vopak employees across eight entities in Singapore, Indonesia, Vietnam, Australia and India.

f.   As part of its expansion plan, Vodafone Group Plc plans to spend around US$ 1 billion to upgrade its network services and retail stores in India as it counts on surging data use to drive growth in the market. Vodafone has 169 million customers in India and posted Rs 376 billion (US$ 6.08 billion) in service revenue in FY 2013-14.

Government Initiatives

Plans to double India's exports of goods and services by the end of the 12th Five-Year Plan period, over the level achieved at the end of the 11th Five-Year Plan period is clearly outlined. For a long term, the   objective is to double India's share in global trade by the end of 2020 through adoption of appropriate strategies. A host of initiatives from the Government of India has helped to give a big boost to India's global trade. These are highlighted as follows:

1. The Reserve Bank of India (RBI) has eased the guidelines for issue of shares or convertible debentures under the automatic route which will allow companies to issue equity shares to a resident outside India against any type of fund. The norms allow issuance of shares subject to conditions such as entry route, sectoral cap, pricing guidelines, and compliance with the applicable tax laws.

2. In line with Government's 'Look East Policy', Shipping Corporation of India (SCI) has started a fortnightly service to Myanmar. The service will cater to Mizoram and other north-eastern states using the Sittwe port in Myanmar located on the mouth of the Kaladan river.

3. The Government of India has signed the Free Trade Agreement (FTA) with the 10-member Association of Southeast Asian Nations (ASEAN). This move is expected to pave the way for freer movement of professionals and further open up opportunities for

investments. Trade between India and the 10-member bloc stood at about US$ 76 billion in 2012-13. The aim of both sides is to increase it to US$ 100 billion by 2015 and envisage lifting import tariffs on more than 80 per cent of traded products by 2016.

Study

A study on the basis of following questionnaire [(*Services marketing checklist (Berry & Parasuraman]*)was conducted on students of MBA 2013-15-Sem IV who were on the verge completing their course at my Institute. The study has tried to come out with qualitative as well as quantitative aspects with respect to services marketing. The class of 78 students was asked to fill a questionnaire emailed to them to be filled and returned to me via email in one week. Out of 78, only 25 replied with completely filled questionnaire without any pressure exerted from my side. I did not ask others to fill and email the questionnaire back to me as I was not interested in any uninterested participants in my study. The questionnaire with its summarized findings is as follows.

Questionnaire based on a services marketing checklist (Berry & Parasuraman)with its

*summarized findings**

1. Are the service providers presenting   a realistic picture of their services to you ?

    a. Yes   14(M8F6) b. No   11(M7F4)

2. Is performing the service right the first time a top priority for the service provider?

    a. Yes   20(M17F)3 b. No   05(M2F3)

3. Are the service providers communicating effectively with you ?

    a. Yes   14(M12F2) b. No   11(M8F3)

4. Are the service providers surprising you during the service process ?

a. Yes   08(M6F2) b. No   17(M10F7)

5. If yes, reasons

    a. if yes, reasons- They can improvement in their service provide process and they can do Expanding promotion activity with their client.

    b. If yes, reasons : In some cases, I've been happily surprised. Example. 1. Flipkart delivering goods on even Sundays. 2. BSNL technician's quick response to complaints

    c. If yes, reasons: they sometimes include unique way of delivering services

    d. If yes, reasons: their behavior changes when we come across difficult problems

    e. If yes, reasons : additional service charges which we did not aware

    f. If yes, reasons. Sometimes the service providing is very good and even better than we expect in some of the areas, while in some cases, it seems not to be good as perceived

    g. If yes, reasons

Many technical things which we do not try to understand or miscommunicated by Service provider we get know after some time during service process . Like in Warranty technicalities and many things

    h. If yes, reasons

    (1) Threat of substitutes

    (2) To build customer loyalty

6. If No, reasons

    a. No, I have faced no such problem or have heard of anyone facing it.

    b. Most service providers still use traditional methods of performing tasks which are known by everyone so it do not surprise me.

c. they are providing services they are claiming to provide in the same price

d. There is no uniqueness in the delivery of the service process

e. they act normally sometime they surprise us with their hidden n charges

f. no specific reason

g. because it is as per the expectations.

h. they provide service which are expected from them

i. The process is same for everyone every time. Change in service provider should not be changing the output of a standardized process

j. just the expected service or even poor service

k. they provide service which are expected from them

l. they provide service which are expected from them

m. Not Communicating Effectively

n. Service providers are presenting realistic picture of their services while elaborating about it before providing the service.

o. never happened with me

(Neither y nor n=3)

7. Do the employees of service providers regard your problems related to their services as opportunities to make a positive impact on you by solving your problems ?

a. Yes   19(M12F7) b. No   06(M5F1)

8. Do you see the service providers continuously evaluating and improving their performance with respect to your expectations ?

a. Yes   14(M12F2) b. No   10(M5F5)   No reply   1(M0F1)

- M=Male F=Female

Analysis

Following sets of hypothesis were made

1. **Ho**: Perception of realistic service by service providers is independent of gender of consumers

   H1: Perception of realistic service by service providers is not independent of gender of consumers

2. **Ho**: Perception of performing the service right the first time a top priority by service providers is independent of gender of consumers

   H1: Perception of performing the service right the first time a top priority by service providers is not independent of gender of consumers

3. **Ho**: Perception of service providers communicating effectively is independent of gender of consumers

   H1: Perception of service providers communicating effectively is not

   independent of gender of consumers

4. **H0**: Perception of service providers surprising consumers during the service process is independent of gender of consumers

   H1: Perception of service providers surprising consumers during the service process is not independent of gender of consumers

5. **H0**: Perception of employees of service providers regard consumer problems related to their services as opportunities to make a positive impact on consumers by solving their problems is independent of gender of consumers

H1: Perception of employees of service providers regard consumer problems related to their services as opportunities to make a positive impact on consumers by solving their problems is not independent of gender of consumers

6. **H0**: Perception of service providers continuously evaluating and improving their performance with respect to consumer expectations is independent of gender of consumers

    H1: Perception of service providers continuously evaluating and improving their performance with respect to consumer expectations is not independent of gender of consumers

Hypothesis Testing

1. **Ho**: Perception of realistic service by service providers is independent of gender of consumers

    H1: Perception of realistic service by service providers is not independent of gender of consumers

    Chi Square Test

G	REALISTIC	SERVICE	PICTURE	
E		Yes	No	Total
N	Female	6	4	10
D	Male	8	7	15
ER	Total	14	11	25

Oi	Ei	(Oi-Ei)²	(Oi-Ei)²/Ei
6	10x14/25=5.6	(6-5.6)²=0.16	0.0286
4	10x11/25=4.4	(4-4.4)²=0.16	0.0364
8	15x14/25=8.4	(8-8.4)²=0.16	0.0190
7	15x11/25=6.6	(7-6.6)²=0.16	0.0242
			$\chi^2=\Sigma((Oi-Ei)^2/Ei=0.0182$ **(Calculated)**

Here there are 2 rows and 2 columns so Degree of Freedom=(2-1)(2-1)=1

Assuming Significance level α=0.01 and DoF=1 the Critical Value of χ^2= 6.6349(table value)

Assuming Significance level α=0.05 and DoF=1 the Critical Value of χ^2= 3.841(table value)

χ^2**(Calculated)< χ^2(table value)**

It implies that Null Hypothesis accepted i.e., Perception of realistic service by service providers is independent of gender of consumers

2. **Ho**: Perception of performing the service right the first time a top priority by service providers is independent of gender of consumers

   H1: Perception of performing the service right the first time a top priority by service providers is not independent of gender of consumers

Chi Square Test

G				
E		Yes	No	Total
N	Female	3	3	6
D	Male	17	2	19
ER	Total	20	5	25

Oi	Ei	$(Oi-Ei)^2$	$(Oi-Ei)^2/Ei$
3	6x20/25=4.8	$(3-4.8)^2=3.24$	0.675
3	6x5/25=1.2	$(3-1.2)^2=3.24$	2.7
17	19x20/25=15.2	$(17-15.2)^2=3.24$	0.2131
2	19x5/25=3.8	$(2-3.8)^2=3.24$	0.8526
			$\chi^2=\Sigma((Oi-Ei)^2/Ei=4.4407$ (Calculated)

Here there are 2 rows and 2 columns so Degree of Freedom=(2-1)(2-1)=1

Assuming Significance level α=0.01 and DoF=1 the Critical Value of χ^2= 6.6349(table value)

Assuming Significance level α=0.05 and DoF=1 the Critical Value of χ^2= 3.841(table value)

χ^2(Calculated)< χ^2(table value) at Significance level α=0.01.

It implies that Null Hypothesis is accepted i.e Perception of performing the service right the first time a top priority by service providers is independent of gender of consumers

χ^2(Calculated)> χ^2(table value) at Significance level α=0.05

It implies that Null Hypothesis is not accepted i.e., It is not sure that perception of performing the service right the first time a top priority by service providers is independent of gender of consumers.

3. **Ho**: Perception of service providers communicating effectively is independent of gender of consumers

H1: Perception of service providers communicating effectively is not independent of gender of consumers

Chi Square Test

G				
E		Yes	No	Total
N	Female	12	3	15
D	Male	2	8	10
ER	Total	14	11	25

Oi	Ei	$(Oi-Ei)^2$	$(Oi-Ei)^2/Ei$
12	14x15/25=8.4	$(12-8.4)^2=12.96$	1.5429
3	11x15/25=6.6	$(3-6.6)^2=12.96$	1.9636
2	14x10/25=5.6	$(2-5.6)^2=12.96$	2.3143
8	11x10/25=4.4	$(8-4.4)^2=12.96$	2.9454
			$\chi^2=\Sigma((Oi-Ei)^2/Ei=8.7662$ **(Calculated)**

Here there are 2 rows and 2 columns so Degree of Freedom=(2-1)(2-1)=1

Assuming Significance level α=0.01 and DoF=1 the Critical Value of χ^2= 6.6349(table value)

Assuming Significance level α=0.05 and DoF=1 the Critical Value of χ^2= 3.841(table value)

χ^2**(Calculated) > **χ^2**(table value) at** Significance level α=0.01.

It implies that Null Hypothesis cannot be accepted i.e It cannot be said that perception of service providers communicating effectively is independent of gender of consumers

χ^2**(Calculated) > χ^2(table value) at** Significance level $\alpha=0.05$

It implies that Null Hypothesis cannot be accepted i.e It cannot be said that perception of service providers communicating effectively is independent of gender of consumers

4. **H0**: Perception of service providers surprising consumers during the service process is independent of gender of consumers

   H1: Perception of service providers surprising consumers during the service process is not independent of gender of consumers

Chi Square Test

G				
E		Yes	No	Total
N	Female	6	7	13
D	Male	2	10	12
ER	Total	8	17	25

Oi	Ei	(Oi-Ei)²	(Oi-Ei)²/Ei
6	13x8/25=4.16	(6-4.16)²=3.3856	0.8138
7	13x17/25=8.84	(7-8.84) ²=3.3856	0.3830
2	12x8/25=3.84	(2-3.84)² =3.3856	0.8817

10	12x17/25=8.16	(10-8.16) ²=3.3856	0.4150
			$\chi^2=\Sigma((Oi-Ei)^2/Ei=2.4935$ (Calculated)

Here there are 2 rows and 2 columns so Degree of Freedom=(2-1)(2-1)=1

Assuming Significance level α=0.01 and DoF=1 the Critical Value of χ^2= 6.6349(table value)

Assuming Significance level α=0.05 and DoF=1 the Critical Value of χ^2= 3.841(table value)

χ^2(Calculated)< χ^2(table value)

It implies that Null Hypothesis is accepted i.e., Perception of service providers surprising consumers during the service process is independent of gender of consumers

5. **H0**: Perception of employees of service providers regard consumer problems related to their services as opportunities to make a positive impact on consumers by solving their problems is independent of gender of consumers

   H1: Perception of employees of service providers regard consumer problems related to their services as opportunities to make a positive impact on consumers by solving their problems is not independent of gender of consumers

Chi Square Test

G				
E		Yes	No	Total
N	Female	7	1	8
D	Male	12	5	17
ER	Total	19	06	25

Oi	Ei	$(Oi-Ei)^2$	$(Oi-Ei)^2/Ei$
7	8x19/25=6.08	$(7-6.08)^2=0.8464$	0.1392
1	8x6/25=1.92	$(1-1.92)^2=0.8464$	0.4408
12	17x19/25=12.92	$(12-12.92)^2$ =0.8464	0.0655
5	17x6/25=4.08	$(5-4.08)^2=0.8464$	0.2074
			$\chi^2=\Sigma((Oi-Ei)^2/Ei=0.8529$ (Calculated)

Here there are 2 rows and 2 columns so Degree of Freedom=(2-1)(2-1)=1

Assuming Significance level α=0.01 and DoF=1 the Critical Value of χ^2= 6.6349(table value)

Assuming Significance level α=0.05 and DoF=1 the Critical Value of χ^2= 3.841(table value)

χ^2(Calculated)< χ^2(table value)

It implies that Null Hypothesis is accepted i.e., Perception of employees of service providers regard consumer problems related to their services as opportunities to make a positive impact on consumers by solving their problems is independent of gender of consume

6. **H0**: Perception of service providers continuously evaluating and improving

their performance with respect to consumer expectations is independent of gender of

consumers

H1: Perception of service providers continuously evaluating and improving

their performance with respect to consumer expectations is not independent of gender

of consumers

Chi Square Test

G				
E		Yes	No	Total
N	Female	2	5	7
D	Male	12	5	17
ER	Total	14	10	24*

- One female respondent neither said yes nor said no.

Oi	Ei	$(Oi-Ei)^2$	$(Oi-Ei)^2/Ei$
2	7x14/24=4.08	$(2-4.08)^2=4.3264$	1.060
5	7x10/24=2.92	$(5-2.92)^2=4.3264$	1.482
12	17x14/24=9.92	$(12-9.92)^2=4.3264$	0.4361
5	17x10/24=7.08	$(5-7.08)^2=4.3264$	0.6111
			$\chi^2=\Sigma((Oi-Ei)^2/Ei=3.5892$ (Calculated)

Here there are 2 rows and 2 columns so Degree of Freedom=(2-1)(2-1)=1

Assuming Significance level α=0.01 and DoF=1 the Critical Value of χ²= 6.6349(table value)

Assuming Significance level α=0.05 and DoF=1 the Critical Value of χ²= 3.841(table value)

χ²(Calculated)< χ²(table value)

It implies that Null Hypothesis is accepted i.e., Perception of service providers continuously evaluating and improving their performance with respect to consumer expectations is independent of gender of consumers

Outcome of the sets of the hypothesis as above can be summarized below:

1. Perception of realistic service by service providers is independent of gender of consumers (Assuming Significance level α=0.01 and DoF=1, and Assuming Significance level α=0.05 and DoF=1)

2. **a.** Perception of performing the service right the first time a top priority by service providers is independent of gender of consumers(Assuming Significance level α=0.01 and DoF=1)

   b. It is not sure that perception of performing the service right the first time a

    top priority by service providers is independent of gender of consumers (Assuming Significance level α=0.05 and DoF=1)

3. It cannot be said that perception of service providers communicating effectively is independent of gender of consumers (Assuming Significance level α=0.01 and DoF=1, and Assuming Significance level α=0.05 and DoF=1)

4. Perception of service providers surprising consumers   during the service process is independent of gender of consumers(Assuming Significance level α=0.01 and DoF=1, and Assuming Significance level α=0.05 and DoF=1)

5. Perception of employees of service providers regard consumer problems related to their services as opportunities to make a positive impact on consumers by solving their problems is independent of gender of consume(Assuming Significance level $\alpha=0.01$ and DoF=1, and Assuming Significance level $\alpha=0.05$ and DoF=1)

6. Perception of service providers continuously evaluating and improving their performance with respect to consumer expectations is independent of gender of consumers (Assuming Significance level $\alpha=0.01$ and DoF=1, and Assuming Significance level $\alpha=0.05$ and DoF=1)

Limitations of the study:

a. Very small sample size

b. Respondents may be lacking complete understanding of companies offering services to them

c. Biases for or against companies

REFERENCES

1. Kotler Philip., Keller Kevin., Koshy Abraham., and Jha Mithileshwar, *Marketing Management-A South Asian Prespective* 14e Pearson Education 2013.

2. Cateora Philip R., Grasham John L., and Salwan Prashant, *International Marketing,*13 e , New Delhi: Tata Mc-Graw Hill Publishing Company Limited, 2008

3. Belch George E., Belch Michael A., and Purani Keyoor, *Advertising and Promotion-An Integrated Marketing Communications Perspective* 9 e (SIE) New Delhi, Tata Mc-Graw Hill Education Private Ltd, 2013.

4. Daniels John D, Radebaugh Lee H, Sulivan Daniel P , and Salwan Prashant, *International Business-Environments and Operations* 12 e Pearson Education ,2010.

RESEARCH SUPPORT

Dr Mamta Brahmabhatt, Associate Professor , B.K School of Business Management, Gujarat University, Ahmedabad, Gujarat, India.

About the Author

Dr. Prateek Kanchan is B.Sc (Mathematics, Physics, and Chemistry), MBA (Marketing), Ph.D. (Advertising)

Dr. Prateek Kanchan Is Professor and Director, B.K.School of Professional and Management Studies, , Gujarat University, Ahmedabad. His specialization areas include Integrated Marketing Communications, International Marketing, Marketing Management and Consumer Behavior. Dr. Prateek Kanchan has two years of industrial experience and twenty two years of experience in teaching at PG level. He has also presented Thirty One papers at national and international conferences, many of them held at various institutes like IIM-Kolkata, Kozhikode and Indore, to name a few. He also has to his credit an edited book on 'In-Film Advertising-Brand Positioning Strategy' and two reference books titled as 'Contemporary Marketing Promotions' and 'Dynamics of 21st Century Marketing Communications'.

He has to his credit thirty two articles and papers published in various souvenirs, journals, newspapers and newsletters. Under his guidance, 4 Ph.Ds have been awarded and 8 scholars are pursuing Ph.D. He has taken a number of sessions as Key Note speaker, invited speaker and session chair at various academic conferences and seminars nationally and internationally, besides being external examiner to many Ph.D Theses outside Gujarat University. He is always there to motivate teachers and students in higher management education.